Teaching Test-Taking Skills

Teaching Test-Taking Skills

Proven Techniques to Boost Your Student's Scores

GUINEVERE DURHAM

ROWMAN & LITTLEFIELD EDUCATION
Lanham • Toronto • Plymouth, UK

Published in the United States of America
by Rowman & Littlefield Education
A Division of Rowman & Littlefield Publishers, Inc.
A wholly owned subsidiary of The Rowman & Littlefield Publishing Group, Inc.
4501 Forbes Boulevard, Suite 200, Lanham, Maryland 20706
www.rowmaneducation.com

Estover Road
Plymouth PL6 7PY
United Kingdom

Portions of chapters 1, 5, 6, 10, 13, 14, 19, 20, 21, and appendix A are adapted or reprinted from Guinevere Durham, *Surviving Today's Schools: The Inside Story* (Baltimore: Publish America, 2003). Used with permission.

British Library Cataloguing in Publication Information Available

Library of Congress Cataloging-in-Publication Data

Durham, Guinevere, 1937–
Teaching test-taking skills : proven techniques to boost your student's scores / Guinevere Durham.
p. cm.
Includes bibliographical references.
ISBN-13: 978-1-57886-572-7 (hardback : alk. paper)
ISBN-10: 1-57886-572-7 (hardback : alk. paper)
ISBN-13: 978-1-57886-573-4 (pbk. : alk. paper)
ISBN-10: 1-57886-573-5 (pbk. : alk. paper)
1. Test-taking skills—Study and teaching. 2. Educational tests and measurements. I. Title.
LB3060.57.D87 2007
371.26—dc22 2006033814

Contents

I

CONCEPTS

1

Test-Wiseness: What, When, Why, and How

The word *test* generates physical, mental, and emotional reactions in people who hear it and have to comply. These reactions are magnified in the students in our schools.

According to Divine and Kylen, three factors have a bearing on how well one does on a test: "1.) Knowledge of the material, 2.) Test anxiety, and 3.) Test-wiseness" (1979, vi). As for the first item, I have found that the vast majority of teachers are dedicated professionals who effectively teach the knowledge of skills.

The second factor, test anxiety, is familiar to all of us. The physical ailments are the most obvious: sweaty palms, butterflies in the stomach, headaches, loss of appetite or excess appetite, and loss of sleep. Then there is the worry factor. Bright students worry about maintaining their As and their rank in the class, while struggling students worry about passing. They all worry about what would happen if they forgot everything and did poorly.

The third factor, test-wiseness, is the set of past experiences and techniques that the test taker brings to the test. It is also the person's familiarity with the format of the test. Elementary school children, being new to the testing situation, have not had the opportunity to acquire test-wiseness.

The purpose of this book is to provide teachers with the theory, strategies, and techniques effective in teaching test-wiseness, referred to in this book as test-taking skills. When I was a first-year teacher, my principal instilled in me the adage "do not assume." This book is written with that in mind: do not assume that your students know how to take a test. Many studies have been conducted that verify the necessity of teaching test-taking skills to students.

1. Eugene A. Jongsma and Elaine Warshauer studied effects of test-wiseness programs on reading achievement test scores. "Test-wiseness exists and can be measured, appears to comprise specific skills, and can be taught effectively. Both low achievers and high achievers who received instruction got higher average scores than their counterparts in a control group" (Lang, 1981, 741). Higher scores ranged from three to eight months.
2. Scruggs and Mastropieri stated, "In our own research on standardized tests, we have found that gains of 10 to 15 percentile points or six months of school achievement are common and that some individual gains are much greater" (1992, 7).
3. Bernard Feder stated that "the ability to perform well on tests is not only an educational accomplishment, but a social and psychological one as well. The successful test-taker . . . builds a positive self-image and a foundation of confidence that help to shape the future. Conversely, failure to do well feeds upon itself" (1979, 1–2).

This research was innovative at the time. Today it is even more relevant. By teaching test-taking skills, we can help students overcome test anxiety so that their test results will be a true assessment of their knowledge of the skills. This book will demonstrate how to teach test-taking skills throughout the school year using this material in conjunction with the textbooks and other curricular material required by your school system.

Teach this acronym to students and remind them to repeat it in their minds before and during each test: WATCH.

Watch the signs, particularly in math.
Allow enough time; that is, pace yourself.
Two directions: listen and read twice.
Check key words.
Hop over what you don't know. Remember to come back to it later.

2

The Five Categories of Tests

There are five types of test items that are basic to any test, whether teacher made or commercially made. Every test will not contain all five, but students need to know how to deal with each type. Teachers are familiar with each type of test item, but in this age of accountability, students need to become equally familiar with them. When selecting or creating testing materials, vary the format to give students practice in and familiarity with the performance procedures needed for each type of item.

MULTIPLE CHOICE

This is a test that emphasizes recognition of information. Only information that can be written with one correct answer and three challenging distracters is able to be tested in this format. Items tested are facts, dates, places, and names. The following are examples of this type of question:

What is the opposite of *up*?

O several
O wrong
O down
O funny

Jack heard a loud noise. He looked around. It was coming from the woods behind the house. He quickly ran inside. What did Jack hear?

O a tree
O the TV
O nothing
O a sound

ALTERNATE RESPONSE

The student taking this type of test chooses between two possible answer choices. The selection comes in the format of true/false, yes/no, or right/wrong. Factual information is tested using this type of question. The following are examples of alternate-response questions:

The opposite of *go* is *stop*.	True	False
The United States is a country.	Right	Wrong
Ice is hot.	Yes	No

MATCHING

In this type of test, students match information in one column to corresponding information in a parallel column. The information tested is primarily recognition of names, dates, numbers, terms, definitions, and specific applications. The following are examples of matching questions:

A. cat	__ a color
B. apple	__ an animal
C. red	__ a flower
D. tulip	__ a fruit

COMPLETION

In a completion question, the test taker is required to fill in the missing word or words in a sentence. This assesses the test taker's ability to recall information and to use context in determining information. The following are examples of completion questions:

pencil flew coat sailed

1. The boat __________ on the lake.
2. I wrote my spelling words with a __________.
3. Jane wore a __________ to keep warm.
4. The bird __________ over the house.

ESSAY

The student is tested on the ability to use written skills to give information. Expository and narrative formats are used for this purpose. The skills that are tested are logical reasoning, sequencing, expression of ideas, organization of material, ability to follow directions, and use of English grammar. As concerns about students' writing skills are becoming more prevalent in the twenty-first century, essay tests are used regularly by school systems as benchmark criteria for promotion, graduation, and accountability.

The expository or open-ended format requires students to respond to a *why* or *how* question. The finished essay will explain, inform, define, or instruct through facts, examples, and sequential steps. The following are examples of expository essay questions:

1. Everyone has a preferred way in which to spend his or her free time. Think about your favorite hobby or activity. Explain why this is your favorite pastime.
2. A new student enrolls in your school and wants to know the rules of a game played at recess. Think about your favorite game. Write directions that will explain to the new student how the game is played.

The narrative or on-demand format requires the student to write about something that has happened or to write a sequential story on a specific topic. The following are examples of narrative essay questions:

1. Birthdays are special times for everyone. Think about a birthday in your family that you will always remember. Write about what happened on this occasion.
2. When you arrived home from school, a large box was sitting near the front door. Write a story about the box and its contents.

Chapter 20 explains in more detail both the criteria used and the scoring of writing tests. Sample test questions are also listed there.

TEST DIRECTION VOCABULARY

Children may have difficulty understanding that instructions for a specific task can sometimes be stated in different ways. For example, test instructions use many different commands to tell students to designate the answer: *mark*, *bubble in*, *fill in*, *blacken*, *color in*, *shade*, and *darken*. Children may know how to draw a line under a word but may be thoroughly confused when the directions tell them to select a word that means the same as the underlined word.

Students may prepare for tests by reviewing the material taught in the classroom; by not cramming, which can cause confusion, fatigue, and uncertainty; and by getting adequate rest and nourishment. The next step for students, both before and during a test, is to understand the test directions. Before taking a test, students should become familiar with the following test direction words and their meanings. During the test, they should raise their hand and ask for clarification if needed. In standardized tests, however, the test directions often do not permit clarifications.

To help students become familiar with test direction vocabulary, make signs of the three most important directions and post them in your classroom, referring to them often. These signs should use direction words specific to the test or tests used by your school system. Examples of test directions are as follows:

Stop Wait Go on

Direction vocabulary words can be categorized by the type of test in which they are used. As new federal and state tests are developed, note the direction vocabulary used on them and add those terms to the following lists.

General

circle, space, oval, shape
row
not
not true, false
sample
best
box
probably
only
diagram
corresponding space
key words

Reading

passage, story, paragraph, phrase, selection, item
in this story, refers to, to this passage
main idea, mainly about, all about
sounds like, rhymes with
goes with
underlined word, underlined letters
describes, tells about
punctuation
opposite, synonym, antonym
sequence, order in which things happen
compare, contrast, similar, the same
cause, effect

Math

General

figure, shape, circle
shade, shaded (usually referring to fractional parts of a whole)
problem, item
equal to, equivalent, another name for
empty set, belonging to a set
solve, work the problem

Addition

altogether
in all
total
how many, how much
join
how much

Subtraction

how many (much) more
how many (much) less
difference
how many are left
most/more
least/less

Multiplication

times
each
how many in all

Division

what fraction, what part

divided into
divided equally
each, how many in one
average

Miscellaneous

beginning, middle, end, next, finally, last
top, bottom
before, after
over, under, above, below
choice
none, none of these, none of the above, not here
in real life, cannot really happen
diagram, table, chart, graph
makes sense
bold face, italics, dark print
best tells
stands for, the same as, another way of saying, almost the same as, closest in meaning to, refers to
next to, next
down

As your students take federal or state standardized tests, note the format and testing directions. Use this same format in teacher-made tests throughout the school year. Incorporate the test directions into the everyday instructions for classwork and homework.

The testing assessment coordinator for your school system may be able to provide extra blank scoring bubble sheets (sample in appendix B). Use several different formats of answer grids so students will become familiar with reading a test and marking the answers on a separate answer sheet. Kindergarten through third-grade students mark in their consumable test booklets. The above practice is especially beneficial in fourth grade, when separate answer sheets are used for the first time.

The materials to use for the lessons are whatever textbooks, trade books, or workbooks the school board has adopted for classroom use. When teaching skills for reading comprehension tests, use passages from the textbooks of the previous grade level or from material used earlier in the school year. When learning a new test-taking skill, the student needs to concentrate on that skill alone, thus the purpose of using an independent level of reading material. Once the test-taking skill is mastered, use more difficult material to prepare the student for actual teacher-made tests and those required by the school system.

II

COMPUTATION

3

Construction of Test Items

SEVEN KEY DEFINITIONS

Should you wish to construct your own tests for your students, you will find it helpful to understand the terms for the parts of the answers and questions. According to the Florida Department of Education *Item Development Workshop* booklet, the definitions are as follows:

1. Key: The correct answer in multiple choice
2. Options: Possible choices for answers in multiple choice
3. Response: Examinee's choice for an answer
4. Stem: The question
5. Stimulus: Material student reacts to in selecting the best answer
6. Distractor: Incorrect answer
7. Foil: Incorrect answer (1981, 8)

According to Burrill, "The question, or stem, must state clearly what is being asked; the correct answer must be clear and unambiguous and the incorrect choices (distractors) must be both attractive to the examinee who does not know the answer and clearly incorrect to the examinee who does know the answer" (Burrill, 1981, 2).

SEVEN WRITING GUIDELINES

When constructing teacher-made tests, the following seven guidelines, samples, and examples will help you to ensure that the test items are closely aligned with those found in commercially made tests. These guidelines were presented in the Item Development Workshop (see Florida Department of Education, 1981, 2) in which I participated when writing test items for the Florida State Student Assessment Test in reading. The rules are theirs; the examples are mine. Remember that tests are given to assess information as straightforwardly as possible. They are not intended to trick the student.

1. The answer choices should contain only one best or correct response.

Example:

Joe saw a white rabbit in the backyard. The rabbit hopped all around the yard. Then it went into a hole near the fence. The rabbit was:

The following choices are poorly written; two answers could be correct.

O in a box
O in a hole
O in the yard
O at school

The following choices are better. There is only one possible response.

O in a box
O in the house
O in the yard
O at school

2. The grammar must be consistent.

Example:

The elephants walked around the circus ring. Each elephant used its tail to hold the tail of the elephant in front of it. A pretty girl rode the first elephant. Who rode the elephant?

The following choices are correctly written; all are nouns.

O a girl
O an elephant
O a boy
O a monkey

The choices in the following question are correctly written as well; all begin with past-tense verbs.

The elephants

O knocked down the tent.
O sat down.
O walked around the ring.
O stood still.

The choices in the following question are poorly written. The responses begin with different parts of speech.

What did each elephant hold in its trunk?

O moving wagons
O a tail
O a log
O tightly

3. Do not give the answer in a previous question or response.

Example:

Bill rode his bike to school. It began to rain. Bill got wet. After he got to school, he called his mom to bring him dry clothes.

What did Bill ride?

O the school bus
O a bike

O a horse
O a truck

Where did Bill ride his bike?
O to a park
O in a parade
O to school
O to his house

The second question is poorly written because it gives the answer to the first question.

4. Ask one clear question in the simplest language.

Example:

Read the story. Choose the sentence that tells what happened.

Fred walked through the lunch line. He dropped his tray. There was food all over the floor.
O Fred dropped his tray.
O Fred mopped up the floor.
O Fred ate his food.
O Fred did his homework.

The first answer choice is correct. However, the student might take "what happened" to mean "what happened next" and choose the second response.

The following is another example:

In our class there are 10 boys and 12 girls. Today two students were absent. How many boys and girls were there altogether?
O 10
O 12
O 20
O 22

This question is poorly written. Is it asking how many boys and girls are usually in the class or how many are in the class today?

5. Put as much wording as possible in the question, but only the facts.
Example:

Mother and Sally went shopping. They bought some red shoes. Sally wore the new shoes home. What did they buy?

O They bought some shoes.
O They bought some candy.
O They bought a dog.
O They bought some socks.

The answer choices should be written in simplest form: shoes, candy, a dog, socks. Unnecessary wording is confusing to students.

6. Put no irrelevant material in the stem or the response.
Example:

My new shirt has stars on the front. Count the stars.

* * * * *

O 2
O 5
O 9
O 11

This is a math problem, not a reading question. "My new shirt has stars on the front" is irrelevant.

7. Vary the position of the responses. Do not put the answers in a pattern.
The following arrangement of answers is not good: 1. A, 2. B, 3. C, 4. A, 5. B, 6. C, 7. A, 8. B, 9. C. A random arrangement of answers, such as 1. A, 2. C, 3. A, 4. B, 5. C, 6. A, 7. C, 8. B, 9. B, is better.

4

Weekly Format and Sample Lesson Plans

Select the skill of the week, for example, main idea, sequence, or cause and effect. Then select material (preferably previously learned) from the classroom textbooks that you will use to teach the skill. The skill or skills will remain the same all week. Students may take two to three weeks to achieve mastery of the more complex test-taking skills (chapters 6 to 14).

Appendix E contains a summary of this weekly plan format, and appendix F contains a blank daily lesson plan form that may be copied, easily filled in with the material for the week's lessons, and clipped to your plan book. A sample lesson plan for a week is provided at the end of this chapter.

MONDAY

While the students are reading the passage, write the questions and four answer choices on the board or display them using an overhead projector. Putting the sample questions on a transparency or saving them in your computer will allow them to be shared with other teachers and saved for use in subsequent years.

The questions must be written in test format, that is, with each question having four answer choices. Remember to put a bubble in front of or underneath each answer choice.

After they read the passage and the questions, students should jot their answers on paper. Discuss the question with students, and identify the correct response by pinpointing the facts in the passage. Then discuss the three incorrect choices, and, again, identify why they are incorrect by locating the material in the passage or noting material that is not in the passage. (See chapter 11 for more detailed strategies for choosing the correct answer for multiple-choice questions.) Once the class selects the correct answer, ask one student to go to the board or to the overhead projector and actually bubble in the response.

Examples:

1. The main idea of the story is:
   A. (an answer completely off target)
   B. (the main idea of one page or paragraph, but not of the entire passage)
   C. (a statement about one unimportant fact in the selection)
   D. (the correct answer)

2. The (effect) happened because (cause).
   A. (a factual statement about a previous story)
   B. (a statement about the effect)
   C. (a statement about the cause, but not the cause itself)
   D. (the correct answer)

TUESDAY

Repeat the format of Monday's lesson, using a different selection.

WEDNESDAY AND THURSDAY

Repeat the format of Monday's and Tuesday's lessons, but guide students toward selecting the correct and incorrect responses and documenting their choices. As a homework assignment or classroom practice activity, assign each student specific pages of the material being worked on in class. The students will read the pages and then write one test question with four answer choices. This is graded as any other homework assignment. You will later use some of these as actual questions on the teacher-made test.

FRIDAY

Assign students the material to read. Use your preferred method of presentation to display two test questions. The students will answer the questions independently on paper and turn in their responses to you with no discussion about response choices. The grade will not be recorded in the grade book but will indicate to the students and teacher whether or not the material is being mastered. Discuss the correct answers after you have checked the papers and handed them back to the students.

Once the students know that the scores on the tests will not be recorded in the grade book, their test anxiety will be alleviated and they will concentrate on learning the test-taking skill. Stress to the students that these test questions are important learning experiences, not just another graded paper.

SAMPLE WEEKLY LESSON PLAN

The following is an example of a week's lessons. For your purposes, select a passage from the students' textbook. Your task is then to write one test item for each day's activity. For example, the test directions would tell students to read the following passage.

> Did you know that chocolate grows on trees? Over 2000 years ago, the cacao (pronounced kah KOW) tree was discovered in the rainforests in the Americas. Chocolate is made from seeds that grow in pods on cacao trees.
>
> The ancient Mexicans were the first people known to make chocolate. They ground up the seeds and made a tasty drink. In the early 1500s, Spanish explorers came to Mexico and tasted the drink. They liked it very much. They took some seeds back to Spain.
>
> Within 100 years, the chocolate drink became a favorite all over Europe. In fact, some German people made a machine to make

chocolate candy. They took this machine to the United States in 1893 to show at the Chicago World's Fair.

A young man named Milton Hershey saw the machine, liked the chocolate, and bought one of the machines. He brought the machine to his hometown in Darry Church, Pennsylvania. In 1905 he opened the Hershey Chocolate Manufacturing Plant and made chocolate candy. It is now the largest chocolate candy manufacturing plant in the world.

Monday's Lesson

What is the best title for this story?

O The Uses of Chocolate
O The Discovery of Chocolate Seeds
O The Story of the Cacao Tree
O The History of Chocolate

Tuesday's Lesson

What is the main idea of the last paragraph?

O Milton Hershey liked chocolate.
O Chocolate comes to the United States.
O Darry Church is in Pennsylvania.
O The Hershey bar is 100 years old.

Wednesday's Lesson

What is the main idea of the story?

O All about ancient Mexicans
O All about chocolate
O All about Milton Hershey
O All about the chocolate machine

Thursday's Lesson

Select another passage from the textbook and ask "What is the main idea of the passage?" or "What is the best title for the passage?"

Friday's Lesson

Select yet a different passage from the textbook and ask the same questions. The students select the most appropriate response from the four answer choices that you have written.

III

APPLICATION

5

Techniques: Format Familiarity

Once when I was updating a test-preparation program, I piloted the technical aspects with the fourth graders in my school. I gave each student a blank bubble sheet for the lesson. I then reminded them about the format of the third-grade tests, in which they bubbled in their answers in a consumable test booklet. The students' groans and body language told me their opinions of those tests.

I went on to explain that the procedure was different for fourth grade. Instead of marking in their booklets, they would use a separate answer sheet similar to the ones they had on their desks. Then I told them why it was important for them to learn this procedure. They would practice using the bubble sheets to become comfortable with the format by test-taking time. Their teacher would also be using this type of answer sheet for classroom tests.

For practice, I told them to bubble in the space (oval or circle) of the numbers as I called them out. I started calling out numbers: 2. C, 4. A, 7. B. The reaction of the students completely surprised me. Many frantically waved their hands in the air, and some even yelled, "Wait!" Some students looked around the room to see the reactions of their classmates, and others just sat there with blank looks on their faces. I got the message and stopped the lesson. This format was even more foreign to them than I had imagined. I spent the next twenty minutes exploring the bubble sheet with students and thoroughly explaining every aspect of it. We talked about the purpose of the sheet, the reason for the change to this format, and when they would be expected to use it.

I gave the fourth-grade teachers three different types of blank bubble sheets to use with their students throughout the school year. After the state achievement tests were given in the spring, the teachers shared with me their experiences of watching the students and hearing their comments. The frustration experienced by both teachers and students in previous years was no longer a factor in the test results.

Before a person learns how to drive a car, he or she first needs to become familiar with the technical aspects of the vehicle: how to turn everything off and on, where to put the gas into the car, and the purpose of every pedal and instrument. The same is true for students taking tests. Becoming familiar with the test format, or the technical aspects of the test, will help alleviate test anxiety. Do not skip this lesson. Remember, there will still be a bell curve of test scores in your classroom after students have learned test-taking skills, but each student's score will be a more accurate assessment of his or her potential. These skills will also help students do as well as they are able on written tests they will take for licenses and jobs in the future.

The beginning of the school year is the time for testing techniques to be introduced. Then the skills will need to be reinforced before every test given in class.

UNDERSTANDING THE TEST ITSELF

Ask the curriculum specialist to supply you with the following information on the important standardized tests, or at least get the information a few weeks before each test date. Explain and emphasize the following points about the test:

1. What kind of test is being given? (achievement, assessment, reading, math, or other subject areas)

2. Why is the test being given? (for mastery of chapter or book material, placement into a special program, general information, report card grade, or passing/failing)
3. What type of items are on the test? (essay, matching, completion, multiple choice, or true/false)
4. What will the grade be used for? (pass/fail, subject grades for a report card, or ranking of school in district)
5. Who will get the results? (student, teacher, parent, principal, other school system personnel, school system website, or local newspaper)

MATERIALS NEEDED FOR TESTING

Students need to know at the beginning of the school year the materials required at every testing session: two number-two pencils and a good eraser.

Children will sharpen their pencils to the sharpest point possible; however, insist on a dull point and demonstrate why it is better. First, a sharp point will break easily under the pressure of bubbling in, causing frustration. Second, a dull point is wider and will bubble in each space at a faster rate, thus saving precious time.

BUBBLING IN

Students should be taught to always bubble spaces in from the center out, as shown in the following examples. Scoring machines scan the center of the space when checking the answer.

Many elementary children are meticulous in bubbling in the spaces on their answer sheets and thereby waste time on timed tests. Once the proper bubbling method is innate, students will mark their answers more quickly and move on to the next question. Students should also be taught to erase all other pencil marks, for the scoring machine cannot tell the difference between a stray mark and the correct answer. Give students a chance to practice using machine-readable answer sheets by using them when giving your own tests in class. Appendix B contains a sample answer sheet, or you should be able to get a supply from the director of testing and measurement in your school system.

ACTIVITY

Allow students to become familiar with machine-readable answer sheets before they are used for tests. Since kindergarten through third-grade students mark their answers for standardized tests in the test booklet, this activity is used for fourth grade and above.

Give each child a blank answer sheet. Call out letters and numbers, for example, 1. A, 4. C, and tell students to mark the corresponding space on their answer sheet. When the activity is completed, the darkened spaces will represent a picture or symbol, such as the number 4, a dollar sign, or a sailboat. Ask the students to guess what picture is formed. For additional practice, allow students to create their own pictures.

6

Following Directions

I carefully read the directions of the math computation portion of the yearly standardized test to my first-grade students. This was my first year as a teacher, and I wanted to be sure that I did everything right. As the students began their work, I circulated around the room to make sure everyone was on the correct page. I concentrated on the students who I knew might get confused by the format.

Just minutes before time was up, however, I walked by the desk of Ronnie, my top math student, and gasped. I saw him working diligently, and I could see that he would not finish. He had not understood the directions. Ronnie scored thirty percentile points below his ability, and only because of an unfamiliar format.

This is a simple version of what the math page looked like. The sign indicates the type of problem:

1. +	5. –	9. ×
2. +	6. –	10. ×
3. +	7. –	11. ÷
4. +	8. –	12. ÷

Ronnie, instead of working top to bottom as the numbers indicated, worked as he had been taught in class, from left to right. He finished items 1, 6, 11, 2, 7, 12, and 3. He took so much time working on the division problems that he didn't even get to many of the easier addition and subtraction problems.

The reason many students do not do well on tests is that they, like Ronnie, do not understand the exact directions. According to Alford, "The student must be sure that he understands the directions" (1979, 11). Students become confused when test formats or test directions differ from what they have encountered in the classroom.

Test-taking skills need to be incorporated into students' learning activities from the first day of school. However, parents must be informed as to the procedures used in grading papers. In my school, the teachers, as part of the test-preparation program, all agreed to mark students' daily work as correct only if the student followed the directions exactly. This was explained to the students, and teachers did sample worksheets together with their students.

Parents may choose to follow the same procedure with work done at home after checking with the child's teacher as to policies used at school. Once, a second-grade teacher at my school told students to underline the correct answer on a worksheet. One student circled each answer and received a 0 on the worksheet. The student's mother came storming into my office the next day demanding that the grade be changed to 100 because the answers were all correct. I explained why the grade was 0. The teacher had previously sent home a newsletter to parents explaining the purpose of this lesson. "But the answers are correct!" she repeated. I then asked her whether she preferred that her child receive a 0 on one worksheet now or a low score on a standardized test later because the child did not follow the directions exactly. I told her about Ronnie's experience as an example. She understood and reluctantly agreed.

The following are tips that students should be taught to follow when taking tests:

1. Read the whole test or section before beginning, in order to:
   - Become familiar with the test
   - Check the difficulty of the questions (are they the same throughout, or do they progress from easy to hard?)
   - Get an idea for pacing (how long is the test, and how much time is allowed?)
2. Always pay attention to the sample question in order to:
   - Know exactly how to do the section
   - Identify any key words in the directions
   - Clarify oral directions
3. Ask if you don't understand the directions completely!

ACTIVITIES

These activities can be used to teach students about the importance of following directions.

Classroom Lessons

What Is It? (Primary Grades)

Give students a worksheet containing the game chart found in appendix C and the following directions.

1. Color B–2 blue.
2. Color F–2 and F–6 yellow.
3. Color B–3, B–4, and B–5 red.
4. Color D–2 and D–6 red.
5. Color B–6 blue.
6. Color E–2 and E–6 green.
7. Color F–3 and F–5 purple.
8. Color C–2 and C–6 orange.
9. Color F–4 brown.

What is it? _________

Find the Buried Treasure (Intermediate Grades)

Give students a worksheet containing the game chart found in appendix C and the following directions.

1. In B–2, draw a tree.
2. From that box, go across five boxes and put an *X* there.
3. Go down seven boxes and draw three pieces of gold.
4. Follow the trail of gold pieces to find the buried treasure.
   - Go two boxes to the left and draw a large gold piece.
   - Go up two boxes and draw another gold piece.
   - Go two boxes to the left and draw five little gold pieces.
5. Go to the right one box and then up three boxes. Draw a picture of the shovel that the pirates left.
6. Go three boxes to the left and draw a treasure chest, for this is where the treasure is buried.
7. What box are you in? __________
8. Are you right? __________

Surprise (Primary Grades)

Give students a worksheet entitled *Surprise* that contains the following instructions. Tell them to read the worksheet and follow the directions. (See chapter 13 for a true story of an incident that happened when a teacher used this activity.)

1. Read everything before doing anything.
2. Write your name at the top of the paper.
3. Draw a square at the top of the paper.
4. Circle number 7.
5. Draw a line under your name.
6. Say your name out loud.
7. How old are you? __________
8. Stand up and sit down again.
9. What color do you like best? __________

10. Count to 10 out loud.
11. Do only #1 and #2.

Surprise (Intermediate Grades)

As with the primary grades, give students a worksheet entitled *Surprise* that contains the following instructions. Tell them to read the worksheet and follow the directions.

1. Read everything before doing anything.
2. Write your name in the upper right-hand corner of the paper.
3. Write the date under your name.
4. Draw two small squares in the upper right-hand corner of the page.
5. Write the name of your school at the bottom of the page.
6. Draw a box around the name of your school.
7. Raise your left hand and make a circle in the air.
8. Print your first name backward. __________
9. Stand up and sit down again.
10. Shake hands with the person sitting next to you.
11. Count from 1 to 10 out loud.
12. Write the name of your best friend. __________
13. Now that you have finished reading everything, do only #1 and #2 and turn your paper over on your desk.

Hands-on Activities

1. Play Simon Says.
2. Give students step-by-step directions to create an object using origami, the art of paper folding. (Books containing examples of this art can be found in the library.)
3. Play an activity record, CD, or video for the students, and have them physically follow the oral directions. (This is a great bad-weather-day activity that helps get the wiggles out.)

4. Give students step-by-step directions for an art or craft project. Holidays are prime times to use this activity.
5. Play Gingerbread Man. To do this, read the story *The Gingerbread Man* to the class. Tell the students that the class is going to look for the gingerbread man, for you saw him that morning. You will have already arranged what happens next. Take the children to where you supposedly last saw the gingerbread man. A person or a written note at that spot will tell the class that the gingerbread man left there and went to another location. Continue for a few more stops. I liked it best when a teacher used my office as the last stop. When the students arrived, they asked in unison, "Have you seen the gingerbread man?" I responded, "Yes, he's been waiting for you!" That morning the teacher had brought in enough gingerbread cookies for each child to have one. I had the privilege of passing them out to smiling, surprised children.
6. Follow a recipe. For example, make Jell-O following the directions exactly, and make another box using only cold water.
7. Read a play and make a list of the directions the actors must follow for the play to be a success. (Most basal reading textbooks contain a play written for that grade level.)
8. Have students follow directions for writing a secret message: Put some lemon juice or orange juice in a small jar or bowl. Using a toothpick or the handle of a paintbrush, write a message on a blank sheet of paper by dipping the writing tool in the juice. Let the paper dry for a few hours. Hold the paper up to the light and the message will show. For the secret message to show, the directions must be followed exactly.
9. Send students in teams on a treasure hunt around the school. Give each team the first direction. They will get the next direction at the first stop, and so on. Time, grade level, and facilities dictate the number of stops. Remember to notify the principal that students will be out of the classroom, and obtain prior permission of any other adults involved in the activity.

Written Activities

1. Give students a copy of part of a road map. Start with a map of their town and progress to a state map and a map of the United States. Following your oral directions, students will trace or highlight the path from one site to another. For older students, the directions may be in written form.
2. Use test direction vocabulary words (see chapter 2) in written assignments.
3. Give specific directions for a worksheet or workbook page. Your directions may differ from those written on the page. For example, you might tell students to write only the answer, do the whole problem, circle the answer, or mark the two best choices.
4. Using a worksheet containing a black-line picture, give students specific directions for coloring it. Give oral directions for young children and written directions for older students.
5. Have students create a code for writing a message, for example, A = 1, B = 2, and so forth. Then will they write messages using the codes they created, trade papers and codes, and decipher the messages.
6. Each child gives the directions for his or her favorite recipe. The step-by-step directions may be written by the child or dictated to a parent volunteer or teacher aide. Remember to stress the proper sequence of steps for the recipe. Have the children then illustrate each recipe, and put all the recipes into a book that will be a Mother's Day gift. It will be a treasured cookbook in mom's collection.
7. Give the students a prompt for a writing assignment. Use a prompt that asks how or why or that asks the student to tell a story in the proper sequence. Examples of such prompts include "You arrive home and find an unmarked delivery truck in your driveway. What do you think is in it?" and "Tell about your favorite field trip." Discuss whether or not the students answered what the prompt asked.

7

Guessing: Narrow to Two Choices

Sammy sauntered into the house, opened the refrigerator, and very matter-of-factly said, "We started those tests today. But I didn't know some of the answers and I didn't want to read the rest, so I just marked anything."

How many of us have done that? As adults, we have had to learn how to select an answer on a test when we had absolutely no clue as to the correct answer. We acquired this skill through trial and error. Today's students do not have the luxury of time to learn as we did. The skill of guessing intelligently must be used as early as first grade.

This chapter deals with teaching students two skills: 1) to narrow the choice to two and then guess, and 2) to eliminate all the answers they know are definitely wrong and then guess from what is left.

The first step is to consider the following attributes of the answer choices. If two of the possible answers sound alike, look alike, rhyme, are opposite, have similar meanings, or begin with the same sound, then one of them is probably the answer.

For true/false and yes/no questions, if all the information in the statement is true, then the answer is true. If any part of the statement is false, then the answer is false.

When matching columns of information, the student should match everything he or she knows and then guess from what is left.

When eliminating wrong choices, the student should eliminate every choice that is not stated in the same terms as the question. For example, if the question asks how many days, the student should eliminate responses given in terms of months, weeks, or hours.

The following examples show the process of eliminating incorrect answer choices.

1. Which fruit is red?
   O ketchup
   O apple
   O hot dogs
   O banana

The student should eliminate all items except the red ones and then choose the fruit, or eliminate all items that are not fruit and then select the red one.

2. Mark the answer:

$$\begin{array}{r} 2 \\ 3 \\ +\ 4 \\ \hline \end{array}$$

   O 5 [add 2 + 3]
   O 234 [all three numbers written together instead of added]
   O 9 [correct]
   O 7 [add 3 + 4]

Discuss with students why each of the three wrong choices is inappropriate and should be eliminated.

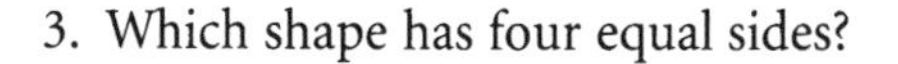

3. Which shape has four equal sides?

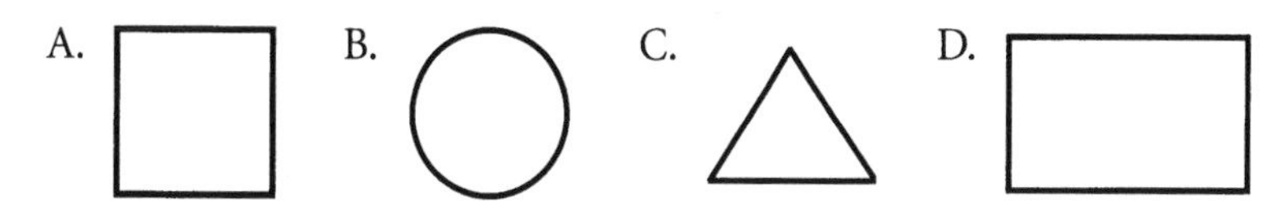

O A
O B
O C
O D

The student should use the key words *four sides* to select choices A and D, and then use the key word *equal* to select A as the correct choice.

ACTIVITIES

Activity 1

The smaller the numbers of choices, the better the chance of getting the correct answer. Play the following game: Write a number from 1 to 50 on a piece of paper, and put the paper face down on a desk. As each student guesses what the number might be, write the guess on the board. After everyone has guessed, show your paper and tally how many students guessed correctly. Do the same activity with numbers from 1 to 25 and 1 to 10. The smaller the number of choices, the greater the chance students have of getting the correct answer.

Activity 2

This activity set is for very concrete learners, but it will help all others as well.

Exercise A

Select four students to stand at the front of the room: two wearing no blue clothing, one wearing a blue shirt, and one wearing blue jeans. Ask, "Which child is wearing a blue shirt?" The students who are seated must first select the students not wearing blue and ask them to sit down, thus narrowing the choice to two selections. Ask the question again. Call on a student to give the correct answer, and then ask why the person wearing blue jeans is not the correct choice. Repeat the activity using other attributes of people or pictures, such as size, shape, height, hair or eye color, things that fly, or things that grow.

Exercise B

Teach the skill of narrowing down the answer choices in a lesson using attribute blocks. Each block in a set has four attributes: color (red, yellow, or blue), size (big or little), shape (circle, square, rectangle, or triangle), and thickness (thin or thick). They can be purchased at a toy, discount, or department store. Put four blocks on a table and ask a student to select a block with a particular attribute. Then ask for another block, this time specifying two attributes. Depending on the cognitive level of the students, increase the selection to three and then four attributes. For example, you might give students these directions:

1. Point to the large blocks.
2. Point to the thin squares.
3. Point to the small, red square.
4. Point to the large, thin, red square.

Exercise C

A fun, challenging game (more so with intermediate students) is to build a train of attribute blocks on the floor of the classroom. Begin by putting the engine (first block) of the train down, and then select a student to add the next car. Say, "Look at the engine. Now select a block that has one attribute [or two, three, or four attributes] different than the engine." For example, if the engine is a large, thick, red square, the student might pick a small, thick, red square. The next student might then pick a small, thick, red circle. When the selection of blocks remaining to choose from lessens in number, the game becomes far more challenging. Allow students to help each other.

Activity 3

Give students a teacher-made worksheet containing several statements important to the reading, science, or social studies chapter that they are currently studying. Have students use the skills they have learned for deciding whether an answer is true or false to write *true* or *false* after each statement. Students should then write the page number in the textbook where the fact is documented.

Activity 4

For homework, assign students a passage to read in any one of their textbooks. They should then write two statements about the passage, one true and one false. Again, students should document the statements with page numbers.

8

Guessing: Judging Answers

"Guess what?" Beth excitedly asked her mom as she burst through the front door. "My friend taught me a new word today, 'Christmas treeing.'" Noting the puzzled look on her mom's face, she continued explaining her revelation. "I don't mean like the one we decorate at Christmastime. We took those long reading tests today, and Sue told me that if you don't feel like reading all that stuff, you can just mark any answer. It's called Christmas treeing. I guess that's because the paper looks like the lights on the tree, with marks all over the page." Beth then proudly stated, "I was the first one done!"

A very upset mom and dad told this story in my office the following morning. Fortunately, the test was not a major assessment but simply a publisher's periodic reading test given after the first section of the reading book was taught. Beth and Sue were allowed to retake the test in the guidance counselor's office, during the time they usually had recess. The entire faculty used this opportunity (without mentioning names or the incident) to discuss with their students why it is so important to read a test and then use the test-taking skills they have learned in order to select the best answer.

When using guessing skills (see chapter 7), some students still may be confused or even overwhelmed by the choices and may have difficulty making the selection. In order to narrow the choice to two or eliminate wrong answers and guess from the remaining choices, the student needs to learn how to evaluate or judge the responses.

Several attributes of the answers that must be considered are:

- ✓ Is the answer written in the same terms as the question? (e.g., feet/yards, dollars/cents, days/weeks)
- ✓ Does the response answer what the question asks? (e.g., *who* = person, *when* = time, *where* = place)
- ✓ Is the response mentioned in the story? (e.g., the story discussed a bike ride, and the answer talks about a car)
- ✓ Does the response satisfy the key words in the question? (e.g., for the question, "What could not really happen?" the answer must be something that could not happen)

ACTIVITIES

1. Play the game Hold Everything. This is particularly effective when used as a review for a test. Select pages in the reading, social studies, or science textbook to be considered. Allow the students to ask you questions about the material. This can be done with open books. Your answers will vary, sometimes being factual and sometimes being fictional or incorrect. When a fictional or incorrect answer is given, students must say aloud, "Hold everything!" Students love this game, and they can get quite loud. Next, reverse the process and ask the students questions. The students will try to outdo each other with the most outrageous answer. However, once the answer is recognized as fictional, the student has to give the correct answer and then verify it by citing the exact page and paragraph in the text.
2. Present a picture from a textbook, magazine, or poster. Discuss what the picture tells you. Lead the students to answers that are factual as well as fictional or incorrect. Again, ask the students to

document their responses. For example, given a picture of a child sitting on the grass holding a bruised knee, with a tricycle tipped over next to him, an incorrect answer would be that the boy looks happy. The documentation would be the tears on his face or the bruised knee.

3. Use old tests to teach the skill of evaluating answers. Let students discuss the merits of each answer choice. This is also the time to point out that they should read every answer choice to make sure their selection is the best one.

9

Working Backward

A substantial portion of the choices on a first-grade assessment test that was used in my school were in the form of pictures. Students had a tendency to select a picture that had at least one object in it that was mentioned in the question. The year I implemented my test-preparation program, the first-grade teachers came to me at the end of the assessment-test week with big smiles rather than their usual demeanor for the end of test week, which was sheer exhaustion and some frustration. All four of the first-grade teachers had observed that their students would point to each picture, either shake or nod their head, move on, and finally select the best answer. They had used their test-taking skills of judging answers, working backward, and guessing.

There are times when a test taker does not know a word or words in the question. The student then has a tendency to just mark any answer. The following activities can be used to teach students to use information in the answer choices to guide them in making their response. This skill is called working backward.

ACTIVITIES

Activity 1

Begin with a concrete example. Show pictures of four people: one man, two women with brown hair, and a woman with gray hair. Ask,

"Which woman has platinum hair?" The responses will vary and will include shrugs, puzzled looks, blank looks, and the question "What does platinum mean?" Lead the students to use the four answer choices to make their selection:

- First, since the question said "woman," eliminate the man.
- Second, the answer must be one woman only, so eliminate the two women with brown hair.
- Third, select the woman with gray hair. The students do not have to know what *platinum* means in order to make a good choice.

Repeat the activity with other attributes of people and objects.

Activity 2

This activity is best explained by displaying the questions and answer choices on the chalkboard or on paper. Display a question such as the following:

What word is the opposite of b _ d?

O run
O big
O pretty
O good

Discuss each answer choice separately. Because students do not know the word in the question, they should let the beginning and ending sounds of the word be a guide as they evaluate the possible answer choices. As students suggest words that mean the opposite of *run*, write the suggestions on the board. Check the list to see whether or not there is one starting with *b* and ending with *d*. Repeat the procedure with each selection. Then, continue with the following examples:

What is the opposite of s _ _ p?

O yes

O open
O hello
O go

Because students do not know the word given in the question, they must look at each of the answer choices and give its opposite (yes—no; open—close, shut; hello—good-bye; go—stop). They can then evaluate the opposites to see which one matches the beginning and ending sounds of the mystery word.

What is the opposite of n _ _ _ t?
O up
O on
O day
O girl

Again, students should look at the answer choices and give the opposite of each one (up—down; on—off, shut; day—night; girl—boy), then choose the word whose opposite matches the beginning and ending sounds of the mystery word.

Point out that sometimes the choice will come down to one of two and guessing will be the only way in which to select the answer. Use choices written at the students' independent reading level so that the students will concentrate on the test-taking skill, not on the academic material.

Activity 3

Play the game *Jeopardy!* as seen on television. This is especially effective when reviewing reading, science, or social studies material. The students will need their textbooks for this activity. The teacher states a fact (an answer), and students must state the corresponding question or must find the exact words on the page that tell what the question should be. The student who correctly says the question will state the next answer, and so on.

Activity 4

Find an old worksheet or test and use correction fluid to hide some words or letters in each question. Then copy the worksheet or test for students to complete using the newly learned skill of working backward.

10

Key Words

I surveyed five classrooms of fifth graders concerning their feelings about taking tests. One of the survey questions was, "I could do better on tests if _____." One girl responded quite honestly, ". . . if I didn't pay so much attention to the boys."

Reliable tests do not have trick questions, as some test takers believe, but they do have important words or phrases that are called key words. It is advantageous for the test taker to become aware of these words and learn how they make reading the questions and selecting the answer understandable.

Elementary school children know what a key is and what it does: it unlocks something. In tests, key words are used to unlock the information in the question to make selecting the answer easier and quicker. Just as your front-door key will unlock only your front door, a key word will unlock only the correct answer.

There are three steps in the process of using key words to help select an answer to a test question:

1. Identify the key word or phrases.
2. Match the key word or phrase to each answer choice.
3. Select the correct answer (using the skills discussed in chapters 7 and 8).

Make a list of key words, and post the list on the classroom wall. Add to the list as more key words and phrases are identified throughout the school year. Words to begin with are *not, always, never, seldom, mostly, more, less, when, where, why, who, what, how, best answer, in all, altogether, have left,* and any other basic words important to the subject matter of the curriculum.

ACTIVITIES

Hands-on Activities

1. Teach students how a key unlocks information, as in a map, a chart, or a mystery novel. On the board, write students' suggestions of what a key opens (door, padlock, jewelry box, car trunk, diary, luggage, etc.). Make a second list of information that can be unlocked. Examples include maps, charts, mystery novels, phonics, context clues, word attack skills, math signs, spelling rules, science procedures, codes, and grammar rules.
2. Have students make their own list of key words to keep for reference when learning testing strategies or when doing classwork. Options for the list include the following:
   - Small spiral notebook (student purchased) that fits easily into the desk or backpack
   - Computer-printed list
   - Index cards: one word or phrase to a card, with cards kept together in a plastic bag, inserted into a recipe box, or held together with a rubber band
   - Booklet made from paper and stapled together
3. Play the game Simon Says. Identify the key words used in the game.
4. Select a mystery story to use in reading class or to read aloud to students. Students will identify keys that help solve the mystery.
5. Using a road map of their town, students will use the key to determine the distance from their house to school or to each other's homes.

6. Have students make an attribute-block train as described in chapter 7, activity 2, exercise C. Have students listen for key attributes when selecting the next car in the train.
7. Have students do an art or craft project. Give directions one step at a time. Students must identify the key word or phrase in each step that tells them what to do to finish the project, for example, *cut*, *paste*, *draw*, and *fold*.
8. Students will read a play and select the key words that tell the actors what to do, where to move, and what facial expressions and tone of voice to use when speaking. Have students act out the play while ignoring these directions. Then have students act out the play following the directions exactly.

Written Activities

1. Have students underline the key words that give directions on their daily homework worksheets.
2. During social studies and science lessons, read the questions at the end of each chapter. Have students identify the key words before answering the questions.
3. Have students read ads from magazines or the local newspaper. Ask them to highlight the key words in the ads that will entice the reader to purchase the product.
4. Have students read a recipe and highlight the key words in the recipe.

11

Selecting Multiple-Choice Answers

Once students have mastered the individual strategies discussed in chapters 7, 8, 9, and 10, the next step is to combine these skills in a logical, sequential order. Elementary school teachers are adept at identifying students who have difficulty transferring material from one genre to another. These are the students who pick out the key words in a math test question, but haven't realized that the same skill is equally effective in reading, social studies, or science tests.

The following technique is for all students, but particularly for those who want test-taking skills put into practical, logical, user-friendly terms. This technique, which needs to be used often and in every area of the curriculum, is called FOCUS. The first step is to verify that the students at your grade level recognize and comprehend all the words in the acronym. Then proceed with the step-by-step strategy.

FOCUS

F—Find Key Words

The student should begin by identifying key words in the question. The most commonly used key words are listed in chapters 2 and 10. Beyond that, each textbook series has words that are indigenous to that particular subject. Add these key words to the basic list. Possible sources to consider are:

- End-of-chapter questions in social studies and science
- Periodic or cumulative tests that accompany the reading textbook
- Word problems in the math textbook
- Teacher-made classroom tests

O—Omit Wrong Answers

First, the student should omit the choices that do not confirm the key words in the question. (See chapter 7.) Next, omit answers that misstate the facts in the passage. (See chapter 8.)

C—Change Directions: Work Backward

Next, the student should identify any answer choices that contain words or phrases beyond his or her recognition or comprehension level. Then, the student should use the context clues in the rest of the answer to determine whether or not this choice may be a possible correct response. (See chapters 8 and 9.)

U—Use Guessing Clues

If only one answer is the logical response, the student should go to the next step, "S," and select and mark the choice. If there is more than one possible answer, the student should make an intelligent guess. (See chapter 7.)

S—Select and Mark the Answer

Correctly and completely mark the answer.

ACTIVITIES

1. Expose the students to the FOCUS technique by including the words from the acronym in classroom spelling and vocabulary tests.
2. When students are off task, stop and say *FOCUS!* and continue with the lesson in progress. The procedure will both remind the

students what they should be doing at the time and reinforce the word.

3. Require students to list or underline the key words in each question in classwork or homework assignments.

SAMPLE TEST ITEMS

Use the following three sample test items as a guide in teaching students to use a step-by-step procedure when taking multiple-choice tests. Lead them to the realization that the same procedure is applicable regardless of the subject matter. For your classroom, select passages from the textbooks in all areas of the grade-level curriculum. Collaborate with your teammates in writing the test items. The school district's testing coordinator may be able to supply you with old tests that may be used for practice.

Sample Reading Test Item

Peanuts grow best in sandy areas where it is warm. President Jimmy Carter grew up on a peanut farm in Georgia. When he was a young boy, his father taught him how to raise peanuts. He sold the peanuts to earn spending money.

Peanuts are sold in many places as snacks. They may be found in candy, ice cream, and snack bars. Peanut butter sandwiches are a favorite for lunch. But there are some people who can't eat peanuts because they get very sick.

There are over 300 uses for peanuts. Peanut oil is used in cooking. Peanuts are also used in making soap, ink, and paint. Peanut butter can even be used to remove gum from your clothes.

What is the main idea of this story?

A. Everybody likes peanuts.
B. President Carter resided on a farm.
C. Peanuts have many uses.
D. Peanuts can grow anywhere.

Use the steps of FOCUS to select the correct answer.

F—Find Key Words: The key words in the question are *main idea.*
O—Omit Wrong Answers: A is a wrong answer. The story stated that some people cannot eat peanuts because they get sick. D is also a wrong answer. The story stated that peanuts grow best in warm, sandy places.
C—Change Direction: Work Backward: In choice B, the student may not understand the word *resided.* Using the context clues in the sentence and working back to the story, the student is able to substitute *lived* for *resided.* B is true according to the story, but it is not what the story is all about, so it is a wrong answer.
U—Use Guessing Clues: A, B, and D have been eliminated as correct answers. Therefore, C is the answer.
S—Select and Mark the Answer: Correctly and completely mark C on the answer sheet.

Sample Social Studies Test Item

In the future, many people will travel in space. Astronauts had to learn how to do many things in a different way. They will teach space travelers what to do.

There is no food or water in space. It has to be brought from earth. Some water has to be recycled so it may be used again. Otherwise the supply may run out. Food is brought in packages or cans. Water is added to some of it before it is heated in a microwave oven. There are foods such as macaroni and cheese, soup, and even cookies. But there are no peanut butter and jelly sandwiches. The bread crumbs would float around and get into the equipment.

Space travelers sleep in bunk beds or sleeping bags. But they have to be attached to the bed or the wall. They don't want to fly around and bump into things.

Some things will be the same. For fun, space travelers may bring CDs and CD players to listen to music. They bring DVDs to watch movies. They even play checkers.

What is the most important way space travel is different from earth travel?

A. Space travel will be more fun.
B. There will be no peanut butter and jelly sandwiches.
C. There are no souvenir stores.
D. Everything you need must be brought with you.

Use the FOCUS procedure to arrive at the best answer.

F—Find Key Words: The key words in the question are *most important* and *different.*
O—Omit Wrong Answers: A is a wrong answer. Space travel may be more fun for some and not for others. This is not most important.
C—Change Direction: Work Backward: Students may not know the word *souvenir* in choice C. The words *no* and *store* are familiar. Buying souvenirs may be fun, but it is not most important. This is a wrong answer.
U—Use Guessing Clues: B and D are left. B is in the story, but it is not most important. This is a wrong answer. As for choice D, if you forget something (e.g., food), you can't go to the store to buy it. This is very important.
S—Select and Mark the Answer: Correctly and completely mark D on the answer sheet.

Sample Math Test Item

Mom baked 60 cookies for the party. The children ate 27 of them. How many were left?

A. 87
B. 33
C. 47
D. not applicable

Use the steps in FOCUS to find the correct answer.

F—Find Key Words: The key words are *were left*. That means the problem is one of subtraction.
O—Omit Wrong Answers: A is the answer if the numbers are added. The problem is subtraction. C is the answer found if the subtraction is done incorrectly:

$$\begin{array}{r} 60 \\ -\ 27 \\ \hline \end{array}$$

$7 - 0 = 7$
$6 - 2 = 4$
This answer would be 47. Therefore, both A and C are wrong answers.
C—Change Direction: Work Backward: In choice D, the student may not know the word *applicable*. However, this might be a possible answer if the other three choices are all wrong.
U—Use Guessing Clues: D is a possibility. But the computation for B needs to be completed: $60 - 27 = 33$. This is the correct answer to the subtraction problem.
S—Select and Mark the Answer: Correctly and completely mark B on the answer sheet.

12

Pacing

A first-year teacher of second graders worked diligently teaching her students test-taking skills. Before the yearly standardized assessment test, she read the manual twice, rearranged the furniture in her classroom, took down charts that might be advantageous to her students, reviewed what materials the students would need, and finally retaught her students how to bubble in answers. At the end of the first day of testing, she came to me in tears. Her students were being so meticulous in the process of bubbling in the correct answer that they did not finish the test in the time allotted.

The next morning, before she passed out the tests, she discussed this with her students. She used the current terminology and told them that she had stressed it too much. She said, "Be cool! Bubble in and move on!" The students heeded her advice.

Standardized tests have a component not often found in a classroom: time limits. There is no opportunity for the student to finish the work later in the day or to take it home for homework. Students not taught pacing skills tend to either work at a carelessly fast pace or ignore the time restraints and turn in unfinished papers.

The following activities will help students develop an accurate concept of time, thus alleviating test anxiety and resulting in test scores that correctly indicate their skill level.

ACTIVITIES

Concrete Activities

1. Use the math timed test that is found at the end of this chapter. Discuss the activity with the class.
2. Cover the classroom clocks for the day. Students who wear watches will need to remove them for this lesson. Throughout the day, stop and allow students to guess what time it is. Repeat this activity periodically.
3. Give the students five minutes to talk, play a game, or work on a fun project. Do this activity on a day when the clocks are covered. Tell them that they have five minutes, and after the time is up, discuss their concept of the time period.
4. Do the same thing as in activity 3, but assign a tedious written worksheet. Again discuss their concept of time.
5. Using a chart, have students create a list of activities that would require pacing. Some examples are a race, a sporting event, a swimming competition, the student lunch period, the time needed to get to an appointment or to school, meal preparation, and a TV program. Discuss the importance of pacing in each situation. Post the list on the classroom wall and add to it as students discover more activities that need to be done in a specific time frame.
6. Have students calculate the number of problems that will need to be completed in the allotted time in order to finish a math worksheet. For example, to finish fifteen problems in half an hour, two minutes are allotted per problem.
7. Before each activity done in the classroom, allow students to estimate the time required for the task. Discuss criteria for making this judgment: a) the number of problems or questions that are included in the task or worksheet; b) whether the task requires filling in blanks, writing a word or phrase, or writing complete sentences; c) in math, whether the student must show all work or write only the answer; d) whether the subject is an easy or hard

subject for the student; e) whether the student feels prepared; f) how tired the student is (is it morning or afternoon?); and g) whether there are distractions in the room.

Written Activities

1. Time homework assignments. Send home a flyer to parents with directions as to how to do this with homework and household chore assignments. Begin by allowing much more time than needed. Gradually, lessen the time to a realistic limit for the assignment. In the case of household chores, parents should set the time so that students will have to stay on task and work diligently in order to finish.
2. Assign classwork in which the difficulty level varies throughout the assignment. Time the lesson so the students will have to skip the hard problems in order to finish. Lead them to the conclusion as to why this strategy is advantageous in getting a higher score. Devise a system with them to indicate the number of problems they skipped so they know how many to come back to if time allows. Also, stress that they must check periodically to make sure the number of the problem matches the number on the answer sheet.

TIMED MATH TEST

There are two forms for this computation test. Form A begins with problems that are difficult and progresses to easy ones, and Form B contains the exact same problems, but with the easier ones first. You can make your own similar test using problems from the student textbook.

Give half the class Form A and the other half Form B. Give them three minutes to complete the page. Do not tell the students that there are two forms. Tell them that this is a lesson on how long it takes to finish.

After time is up, ask how many students completed all sixteen problems.

Allow students to compare the two forms, and let them discover why the scores differed. Then lead a discussion as to how students can alleviate this situation and ensure that they complete all the problems they are able to do. Suggest the following techniques:

- ✓ Scan the test before beginning to see if the problems go from easy to hard, left to right, top to bottom, or in a random order.
- ✓ Skip the hard questions, returning to them later if time allows.
- ✓ Use skills learned in guessing for the difficult questions.
- ✓ Use skills learned in working backward to select the answer choice.
- ✓ Double check that the answer choice being bubbled in has the same number as the question.

Math Timed Test: Form A

1. $25 \div 5$	2. $56 \div 8$	3. $45 \div 6$	4. $144 \div 12$
5. $\begin{array}{r} 3 \\ \times 2 \\ \hline \end{array}$	6. $\begin{array}{r} 7 \\ \times 7 \\ \hline \end{array}$	7. $\begin{array}{r} 13 \\ \times 4 \\ \hline \end{array}$	8. $\begin{array}{r} 21 \\ \times 15 \\ \hline \end{array}$
9. $\begin{array}{r} 9 \\ -4 \\ \hline \end{array}$	10. $\begin{array}{r} 7 \\ -2 \\ \hline \end{array}$	11. $\begin{array}{r} 18 \\ -6 \\ \hline \end{array}$	12. $\begin{array}{r} 46 \\ -31 \\ \hline \end{array}$
13. $\begin{array}{r} 3 \\ +4 \\ \hline \end{array}$	14. $\begin{array}{r} 8 \\ +7 \\ \hline \end{array}$	15. $\begin{array}{r} 14 \\ +3 \\ \hline \end{array}$	16. $\begin{array}{r} 37 \\ +19 \\ \hline \end{array}$

Math Timed Test: Form B

1. $\begin{array}{r} 3 \\ +\,4 \\ \hline \end{array}$	2. $\begin{array}{r} 8 \\ +\,7 \\ \hline \end{array}$	3. $\begin{array}{r} 14 \\ +\,3 \\ \hline \end{array}$	4. $\begin{array}{r} 37 \\ +\,19 \\ \hline \end{array}$
5. $\begin{array}{r} 9 \\ -\,4 \\ \hline \end{array}$	6. $\begin{array}{r} 7 \\ -\,2 \\ \hline \end{array}$	7. $\begin{array}{r} 18 \\ -\,6 \\ \hline \end{array}$	8. $\begin{array}{r} 46 \\ -\,31 \\ \hline \end{array}$
9. $\begin{array}{r} 3 \\ \times\,2 \\ \hline \end{array}$	10. $\begin{array}{r} 7 \\ \times\,7 \\ \hline \end{array}$	11. $\begin{array}{r} 13 \\ \times\,4 \\ \hline \end{array}$	12. $\begin{array}{r} 21 \\ \times\,15 \\ \hline \end{array}$
13. $25 \div 5$	14. $56 \div 8$	15. $45 \div 6$	16. $144 \div 12$

13

Math: Key Words, Reading Signs, Estimating

The assistant superintendent of the school system arrived unannounced to observe a fifth-grade teacher who was in contention for the district's Teacher of the Year award. She was just beginning a test-taking skill lesson on following directions. As she passed out the worksheets, she also handed one to the visitor.

She simply said, "Begin now and do what the directions tell you to do." This was the paper used:

1. Read everything before doing anything.
2. Write your name in the upper right-hand corner of the paper.
3. Write the date under your name.
4. Draw two small squares in the upper right-hand corner of the page.
5. Write the name of your school at the bottom of the page.
6. Draw a box around the name of your school.
7. Raise your left hand and make a circle in the air.
8. Print your first name backward. __________
9. Stand up and sit down again.
10. Shake hands with the person sitting next to you.
11. Count from 1 to 10 out loud.
12. Write the name of your best friend. __________

13. Now that you have finished reading everything, do only #1 and #2 and turn your paper over on your desk.

After a few minutes, some giggling was heard, and students began looking around the room to see what everyone else was doing. As the assistant superintendent got to number 7 on the paper, he stopped, scanned the rest of the page, and burst into a hearty laugh. Like all the students except two, he had started working without following the written directions.

For days afterward, the students delighted in talking about the educator who didn't follow directions any better than they did. The lesson stayed with them, and they became adept at following written and oral directions. The assistant superintendent used the incident as a teaching tool when working with his principals.

The math sections of standardized tests present challenges that students do not usually encounter in the classroom. Once the students have learned strategies to deal with these challenges, they can concentrate on the math facts presented in the test.

The first of the three principal challenges is that of using key words related to math terminology, for example, *how much more, how much less*, and *how many in all.* Reading and heeding these words, as listed in chapter 2, will lead the student to the correct function to solve the problem at hand. Both identifying these words and knowing the meaning represented by them are needed in the process of getting the answer.

The second challenge is the ability to budget one's time and pace oneself throughout the timed sections in the area of computation. In a classroom setting, students finish as many problems as time allows, but then they may complete the work later in class or take it home for homework. This is not so in a timed math standardized test. Knowing that the test is timed causes anxiety even in the best of students. By teaching pacing strategies while using the students' required math curriculum, both pacing skills and math computation skills will be strengthened.

The third challenge is that of dealing with several functions in the same subtest, that is, addition, subtraction, multiplication, and division problems on the same page. The anecdote at the beginning of this chapter illustrates the importance of following the exact directions. In this case, math signs must be followed exactly. On a classroom worksheet or textbook page, the same computational skill will generally be used throughout the lesson. Tests, on the other hand, often vary the type of math computation problem within a section. Reading signs is especially important because of the nature of the answer choices on a multiple-choice test. For example:

$$\begin{array}{r} 17 \\ -\ 8 \\ \hline \end{array}$$

O 11 [subtract 8 – 7, then 1 – 0]
O 136 [multiply 8 × 17]
O 25 [add 8 + 17]
O 9 [correct answer]

This skill can be reinforced throughout the daily work by requiring students to compute math problems with varying functions. The important strategy is teaching the awareness of the math function.

Stress the following general tips:

- ✓ Check for the key words.
- ✓ Watch the signs carefully.
- ✓ Ask yourself: Should the answer be smaller or larger than the original numbers?
- ✓ On scrap paper, rewrite problems in familiar format. For example, when given the problem 10 – 5 = ____, rewrite it as

$$\begin{array}{r} 10 \\ -\ 5 \\ \hline \end{array}$$

✓ Follow the sequence of items carefully. Do the numbers go vertically, in columns, or horizontally, in rows?

There are three particular areas in the math section that bear mentioning. These can be taught at your discretion using the school's textbooks. Make worksheets in the testing format when checking for mastery of these skills. Send parents a flyer with directions for these math activities to be practiced at home. They are:

✓ Measurement—liquid and linear; teach through cooking, sewing, woodworking
✓ Money—remember to study the back side of the coins and bills; teach through shopping, allowances, budgeting
✓ Time—clocks with both digital readouts and dials. When first teaching time, ask the child often to state the time on the clock. Use the same format that is used in the oral directions for first and second graders on this portion of the math test.

ACTIVITIES

Estimating Activities

1. Students often need additional school supplies. Use the prices of the items in the school store or from local newspaper ads to estimate what it will cost to purchase these items. Do the same with other items that a child might purchase, such as clothing, CDs, and software.
2. Most schools have book fairs periodically to support the purchase of newly published books. Each student is given a brochure of the items for sale (books, posters, and magazines). After returning to the classroom from their walk-through of viewing the materials, teach the students how to both estimate and calculate the cost of their selections. These lists are taken home to parents who edit the selections and provide money for the

purchases. Before the students go to the library for purchasing, assist them in computing the actual costs of the materials and the amount of change to be received from the money the parent has allowed.

3. Many teachers use commercial book clubs for students to order books and software economically. Follow the same guidelines used in activity 2 for this activity.
4. Use everyday situations to create oral word problems. For example:
   - Our family has two children. If each child brings a lunch three days this week, how many lunches will we need to pack?
   - Three students live in our home. Mom wants to order two number-two pencils for each student for the standardized tests. How many pencils will need to be ordered?
5. Using information from your book fair or book club flyers, create word problems. For example:
   - How much more does [title of a book] cost than [title of another book]?
   - I have $20. I bought [title of a book] and [title of another book]. How much change will I get back?
   - How much less is the least expensive book than the most expensive book?

Pacing Activities

1. Use the activities in chapter 12.
2. Conduct math relay races. Divide the classroom into teams. One person from each team goes to the board. The teacher then states a math problem. The first person to write the correct answer earns a point. The functions used in the problems should be varied so that students practice the skill of being aware of the math sign.

3. Put time limits on some homework and classwork. When beginning this skill, allow more than enough time for all students to finish. Gradually lessen the time allotted.

Sign-Reading Activities

1. While traveling to school or around the school campus, make a list of all the posted signs. In the classroom, discuss the purpose of each and what would happen if people did not do what the sign says.
2. Make a worksheet of the format on a math test. Guide students to see that the answer choices are correct for other functions. That is, the problem may be subtraction, but the answers are given using choices for addition, multiplication, and possibly a combination of the original numbers. Examples:

18 − 7	12 + 4	8 × 3	35 ÷ 5
O 25	O 12	O 24	O 175
O 11	O 7	O 11	O 1
O 18	O 16	O 5	O 40
O 2	O 8	O 38	O 7

3. Create a worksheet of math problems, including the answers. But do not put in the sign. The student's task is to put in the proper sign. For example:

15 ? 7	10 ? 2 = 5
O +	O +
O −	O −
O ×	O ×
O ÷	O ÷

Key Words Activities

1. Make a list of key math words (see chapter 2). Use a chart, a small spiral notebook, or note cards. This may be one list or several, each geared to a particular function. Students should keep the list handy when doing homework or classwork.
2. Create oral word problems using familiar facts. Before computing the problem, students must identify the key words. Examples:
   - Our Little League team has _____ players. Three are absent today. How many are playing today?
   - Our team has _____ players, and the team we are playing has _____ players. How many players are there altogether?
3. On written work, require students to circle or underline the key words.

14

Comprehension

As the third-grade teacher circulated around the classroom during the reading comprehension portion of the yearly standardized assessment test, she noticed that Ken was sitting with his hands folded and a big grin on his face. She walked over to his desk, leaned over, and quietly whispered, "What's the matter? Why aren't you working?"

His grin turned into a smile, and he responded, "That was too much reading, so I guessed just like you taught me." Then he proudly added, "I'm the first one finished!"

Ken's favorite subjects were lunch, recess, and physical education. Putting time and effort into a reading test was not a priority for him at that time. But the real underlying reason for his performance was that he was not a proficient reader and the format of the reading test overwhelmed him.

Sound familiar? Reading and social studies teachers, particularly, worry about students who have shown in their daily work that they have the capabilities for completing these sections of the test but who look at the test format and are overpowered with a sense of defeat.

There are four sequential strategies to practice when working on reading comprehension on any test, whether literature or social studies. In order for these strategies to be used effectively and with confidence, the students need practice, practice, and more practice. This can be done using the student's textbooks. The four strategies are as follows:

1. Read the question first. We all retain more information when we have a purpose for reading.
2. Read the passage twice. These passages will have unfamiliar material, but they are not lengthy, and the allotted time is usually generous.
3. Read the questions and identify the key words. (Refer to chapter 10.)
4. Use guessing strategies (chapters 7, 8, and 9).

In a classroom, after students have read a selection from a textbook, the teacher questions them to check comprehension of the passage. The questions are either factual or critical-thinking questions that expect the student to recall information. Standardized tests, because they are scored electronically, are formatted so that the student selects the correct answer choice from four possibilities. These are two different skills. In the classroom method, the student sends out information to the teacher in the answer to the question. The testing method, in contrast, has three steps: first, the student takes in four pieces of information; second, the student considers (processes) the choices; and third, the student sends out the answer to the question. Being able to answer a question using one of these methods does not always transfer to being able to answer the question using the other method. Elementary school students need to be taught from the concrete to the abstract, thus, they need to be taught both ways.

ACTIVITIES

The best way to teach comprehension is to follow the weekly format described in chapter 4. The concepts generally contained in the reading comprehension portion of a standardized test are main idea, making inferences (a particularly difficult skill), cause and effect, sequence, locating information, getting facts (the easiest concept), and drawing conclusions. The skills in this section of a standardized test, being the most challenging to students, must be a priority in the classroom. Consistent and continuous practice is required.

The following questions are frequently used in the reading comprehension section of a standardized test:

1. Main idea
   - What is the main idea of ___________?
   - What is the best title?
   - What best tells about the story?
   - What is the story mostly about?
   - What is the topic of the story?
2. Author
   - Why did the author write this selection?
   - What was the author's point of view?
   - What was the author's opinion of ___________?
   - How did the author feel about ___________?
   - What did the author mean by ___________?
3. Fantasy versus reality
   - What can happen in real life?
   - What cannot really happen?
   - What could not be true?
4. Sequence
   - What happened first in the story?
   - What happened next/finally/last in the story?
   - What happened just before ___________?
   - What happened just after ___________?
   - Put these sentences in order as they happened in the story.
5. Cause/effect
   - <u>(Effect)</u> happened because <u>(cause)</u>.
   - The main character <u>(effect)</u> because <u>(cause)</u>.

6. Inferences/drawing conclusions
    What did the character/author mean when he or she said __________?
    Why did __________?
    The main character felt (emotion) because __________.
    The mood of the passage was __________.
7. Getting facts
    Where?
    When?
    Who?
    What fact tells __________?

The importance of this activity cannot be stressed enough. Select the reading passage, choose a concept, and write five test questions, one for each day of the week. Remember to select a passage at the students' independent reading level, that is, material the student both reads and understands easily (see example below). In each of the seven areas listed above, assign each student one test question with four answer choices. Compile these to create worksheets used in practicing reading comprehension test-taking skills.

Table 14.1 Reading Levels

Reading Level	*Percent of Comprehension*	*Percent of Word Recognition*
Frustrational	49% or less	89% or less
Instructional	50–89%	90–97%
Independent	90–100%	98–100%

15

Sequencing

As a teacher of first- and second-grade students who had limited writing skills, I often allowed them to give their book reports orally to me or to the class. Many of the reports went as follows: "First . . . and then . . . and then . . . and then. . . . The end." The report was one very long run-on sentence, but the sequence of the story was usually quite accurate.

Students of that age are able to retell the story in sequential order. They also are able to read four sentences about the story (not listed in proper sequence) and number them from one to four in the correct order. However, because of the methods of scoring, standardized tests present the questions on sequencing in a more complex format. This is a step beyond the format used in classrooms.

The following test direction is typical of the format for a question on sequencing.

Choose the correct order of the group of sentences below. On your answer sheet, mark the letter of the sentence order that is correct.

1. Mary put chocolate icing on the cake.
2. Mary got out the cake mix and bowls.
3. Mary put the cake into the oven.
4. Mary mixed the cake and put it into the pan.

A. 3 1 4 2
B. 4 3 2 1
C. 2 4 3 1
D. 2 1 3 4

After reading the directions for a test item of this type, I looked at my students and saw facial expressions that cried out, "Help!" I was more frustrated than they were, for I was allowed to read the directions only once and exactly as they were stated in the testing manual.

My students had learned the skill of sequencing. They could both tell and retell a story from beginning to end in a logical sequence. They could recognize when I told a story out of sequence. They were proud of their mastery of the skill of numbering four sentences in sequential order. But this testing format threw them into a state of complete confusion. A question such as this tests their test-taking skills, not their knowledge of the correct sequence of the events in the passage.

In my second year of teaching, I used this format in every area of my primary-grade curriculum. I put examples on the chalkboard. Sometimes I did this before the lesson when teaching the sequence of the activity, and sometimes the lesson dictated that the question be presented to the students only after the lesson was completed. By test-taking time, the students were familiar with the format and thus only had to deal with the content of the material.

Sequencing is also tested by questions that ask when a particular incident happened in a passage. Understanding the terminology in the question will help students choose the correct answer. The following format is used for this type of question. Remember that students will be selecting an answer from a choice of four possibilities.

✓ What happened before __________?
✓ What happened after __________?

- ✓ What happened next?
- ✓ Where does the story start?
- ✓ Where does the story end?
- ✓ What happened first in the story?
- ✓ What happened last in the story?
- ✓ Which comes first?
- ✓ Which comes last?
- ✓ What happened just before __________?
- ✓ What happened just after __________?
- ✓ What did (name) do before __________?
- ✓ What did (name) do after __________?

There are many key words that will help students select the correct sequence for their answer. Make a chart with three columns: Beginning, Middle, and End. Using the words listed below, ask the students which words tell what could happen at the beginning, middle, or end of a story, and place them in the corresponding column of the chart. Keep in mind that some words may be listed in two sections; they simply tell what could not happen at the beginning or what could not happen at the end of the story.

after
after that
at last
before
begin by
beginning
end(s)
finally
first
in conclusion
last
later
middle

next
second
so
start
third

Pronouns (*he*, *she*, *they*, *we*, *it*) are used only after the noun they represent has already been stated. Thus, sentences with pronouns do not happen first.

ACTIVITIES

1. A quick and easy activity is to recap the day's activities. As the students recall each incident, write it on a sheet of paper. The remainder of this activity can be done in either of two ways:
   - Use only four events. Have students number them 1 through 4. Discuss.
   - List several events and ask students to number them sequentially. Discuss.
2. When students are to leave the classroom for home, lunch, or an activity, line them up a few minutes early. Then ask who is
   - first in line.
   - last in line.
   - standing next to (name).
   - standing before/after (name).
   - standing in front of/behind (name).
   - second, third, fourth, fifth, and so forth.
   - at the beginning/end of the line.
3. As a homework assignment, ask students to write four events that happened in the day's literature, social studies, or science lesson. They will then number the events sequentially. These lists of events can then be used for the daily activities in sequencing. Write them into your weekly lesson plan.

4. This activity is for students in the primary grades. Tell three students to come to the front of the room and line up as follows: (name) is last, (name) is in the middle, and (name) is first. Also use first/second/third, beginning/middle/end, or any other sequential order. Do not give the directions in the proper sequence.

16

Spelling

Knowing the difficulty of the spelling portion of the standardized test, I made some classroom tests in the same format, that is, requiring students to choose the correct spelling out of four choices. When I gave the twenty-word test, I followed the same directions used in the standardized test: saying the word, saying it in a sentence, and repeating the word. By the time I called the sixth word, I noticed that Beth kept looking inside her desk. I walked around the room as I continued dictating the words, wanting to get a better look at what Beth was doing. Three words later, I saw what was happening. She would put her left hand just inside her desk and look at her palm before she marked the correct spelling word.

After the test was finished, I gave the class ten minutes of free time, and then I called Beth to my desk. I told her that I would not count that test, but I would allow her to take it again, this time writing each word. She breathed a sigh of relief. She then explained what happened. She knew her spelling words and could write them correctly, but when she saw them written four different ways, she became very confused and wasn't sure which spelling was correct. So she had written the words she was not sure of on her hand. She had not meant to cheat.

Scores on the spelling portion of standardized tests are not indicative of the student's spelling skills. Rather, they are an indication of the student's understanding of the test format. On a classroom spelling test, the teacher says the word and the student writes it. On a standardized spelling test, not only is the format different, but also the cognitive skill involved is different. The teacher's directions are the same as in the classroom. However, instead of writing the word, the student has to select the correctly spelled word from a choice of four words. Elementary school students, particularly in the primary grades, cannot always make the transition from giving out information (spelling the word on paper) to selecting from information given to them (selecting from four choices). This is easily remedied by creating spelling tests to be given in the classroom in the same format as the standardized test. Students can also be taught to think of the correct spelling before looking at the choices. This eliminates some of the confusion.

The following are examples of standardized spelling test questions.

(picture of a cat)

O cate
O cot
O kat
O cat

(picture of a boat)

O bote
O bot
O boat
O bat

The next format is more difficult and is found on tests for intermediate-grade students. In each of four sentences, one word is underlined, but it is a different word in every sentence. Only one of the four words is spelled incorrectly, and the student has to select which one it is.

Choose the sentence in which the underlined word is spelled incorrectly.

1. The Indians lived on a reservation.
2. We used our motor home as transpertation on our trip.
3. The admission fee to the park was $5.
4. The solution to the math problem was wrong.

ACTIVITIES

1. In intermediate grades, assign students to write each spelling word in a sentence. These may be graded for spelling, grammar, or handwriting. Use these sentences on the spelling tests. Of course, one word in each set of four will be misspelled on the worksheet.
2. Meet with the other teachers on your grade level and compile a list of twenty to twenty-five words that are particularly difficult for the students at that grade level. This is very helpful for teachers new to the grade level. Use the compiled list for extra drills before the standardized tests are given.
3. To share the workload, take turns with other teachers to create spelling tests written in the standardized test format. Alternate the format of your tests from week to week: 1) student writes the word, 2) student chooses the correctly spelled word from four choices, and 3) student chooses the sentence in which the underlined word is spelled correctly.

17

Maps, Graphs, Tables, and Charts

The sixth-grade teacher informed her students that, in two weeks' time, they would have an end-of-chapter social studies test. The students knew what those tests were like, so they diligently completed their homework, read and reread pages in the text, and quizzed each other on details. They knew it would be hard.

When the day arrived, the teacher announced that the test would be given right after lunch. When the students walked back into the classroom from the cafeteria, they noticed that the big United States map was pulled down to cover the test questions that were written on the chalkboard. The teacher told everyone to get out two sheets of paper and a pencil. She even waited while a few students sharpened their pencils.

When everyone was ready, she pulled up the map. On the board, in big letters, was written, "April Fool!" One student summed it up best when he shouted, "Wow! That's the best April Fool's joke I ever had!"

I was a student in that classroom. Even though it was many years ago, I can still visualize the room, still remember where I sat, and can still see the teacher release the map to show those words. Many testing situations, like this experience, are very memorable. Teachers today, having to meet the high standards of society (as we did), now have to give many standardized tests to document their accountability.

Each section of a standardized test contributes to the score on the total battery. Though there are generally only a few questions on a standardized test that include maps, graphs, tables, and charts, these questions are important to the total picture. With the importance of technology in the twenty-first century, the ability to read these visual aids is vital. Examples of them can be found at every grade level and in every area of the curriculum.

A graph is a diagram that can help us compare things. The form of the graph depends on the type of information being represented. There are four types of graphs: line graphs, bar graphs, circle graphs, and pictographs.

A map is a picture of an area; that is, it is a drawing that represents the earth's surface. Maps come in many forms. Primary students begin with picture maps, and intermediate students study road maps, physical maps, political maps, and relief maps.

A table is made of words and numbers and takes up a small space. If the same information were put into words alone, it would take many paragraphs. Tables compare information and are easy to read.

A chart depicts several items, and questions relating to charts require the reader to use the properties of the pictures to tabulate information. Charts are particularly effective with primary students with limited reading skills. They are primarily used in math.

The rest of this chapter will give samples, examples, and concrete activities for each type of visual aid. The students' textbooks or the Internet are the best sources to view or create any of these visual aids.

ACTIVITIES

Bar Graphs

Bar graphs show how different quantities compare to a given source or to each other.

1. As a homework assignment, have students check the kinds of shoes everyone in the house has in the closet. Graph each pair ac-

cording to slip-ons, sneakers, sandals, boots, and shoes with laces. In the classroom, graph the types of shoes each child is wearing.
2. Use a bag of M&Ms for this project. Since the students will eat the candy at the end of the lesson, the number of candy pieces distributed to each student depends on the number of students. The students will graph the number of each color of candy. The results can then be put into a table to see whether the bag has an equal number of each color or to see which colors predominate.
3. For a social studies lesson, assign each student to research the population of three cities in your state. Once the populations are determined, teach students how to put the coordinates on a graph.
4. After a vacation, list the favorite attractions of each family member. Put each choice in the form of a bar graph so that students can see everyone's favorites.

Line Graphs

Line graphs show trends or changes over a period of time or over an area.

1. Graph the student population of each grade level in the school or in each classroom on a particular grade level. The students will research the statistics.
2. Check with the cafeteria manager each day for the number of lunches sold. Graph these numbers for a month. This will indicate to the students what the favorite meals are for the school.
3. Graph the temperature each day for a month, making sure it is taken at the same time of day. Another activity would be to take the temperature every hour the students are in class, for one day only. This graph can have two lines, one for the projected temperature and another for the actual temperature.
4. Graph the snowfall or rainfall for several days. Again, there could be two lines, as in activity 3.

Pictographs

Pictographs use actual pictures to represent the data.

1. Have each student draw a picture of his or her favorite toy on a sticky note. Then they place the sticky notes on the graph (a poster or the chalkboard) according to color. Other pictures, such as animals, favorite foods, fruits, or birds, can be used and can be categorized according to color, size, or category.
2. In March, make a calendar and put either a lion or a lamb on each day. At the end of the month, graph the days of each type. Graphing can also be done with cloudy, sunny, rainy, and snowy days.

Circle (Pie) Graphs

Circle or pie graphs show relationships of parts to a whole, usually in percentages.

1. Calculate the expenses for a vacation or field trip: transportation, gas, entrance fee, meals, hotels, and souvenirs. Add each amount to get the total, and then calculate the percent each amount is of the total. Intermediate students can put these percentages into a pie graph on the computer.
2. Check with the cafeteria to get the numbers of students buying lunch and the number buying only milk. Use total enrollment figures to calculate the number bringing lunch from home. Compute the percentages and put them in a pie graph.

Tables

Tables are charts that contains data about sets of different items.

1. Make a table titled "Report Card Grades." The columns contain the report card grades (A, B, C, D, F, or E, S, N, U, or 95, 90, 85, 80). The rows list the subject areas. Only total numbers of stu-

dents are used, no names. Ask the type of questions about this table that students would encounter on a test. For example:
- How many students received Cs?
- What grade did the most students receive?
- How many more students received Bs than As?

2. Use other information from the school for other tables:
   - lunches sold, for example, hot dogs, spaghetti, hamburgers
   - number of students who go to bed at each of four times (teach tallying)
   - political election data (number of voters per grade level, per precinct, or per state)
   - number of books sold at the book fair (five or six favorite titles and the number sold of each)
   - school population (number of grade levels and number of classrooms per grade level)

Maps

Maps show roads, population density, and land use.

1. Take a walk around the school neighborhood, taking note of where landmarks are located. Then have students make a map of the neighborhood.
2. Tour the neighborhood and, again, make note of the landmarks. Have students make a three-dimensional map at home, using cardboard cartons, Popsicle sticks, blocks, clay, and fabrics.
3. Plan a vacation or field trip. Use an actual road map and highlight the route. When actually traveling, give each student a copy of the necessary part of the map so they can follow the charted path.

Charts

Charts show properties of objects.

1. Using a menu from a local restaurant, ask questions that require students to compute and compare prices.

2. Select five items from the classroom (or use items sold in the school store). Make large price tags for each. As in activity 1, create several addition and subtraction problems using these prices.
3. Display four items: a ball, a book, a triangular block, and a square box. Ask questions that require students to identify properties of the items, for example, shape, number of corners, or number of sides.

EXAMPLES

The following visual aids are examples of the type of items found on standardized tests. Use maps found in social studies textbooks for practice with maps.

Bar Graph

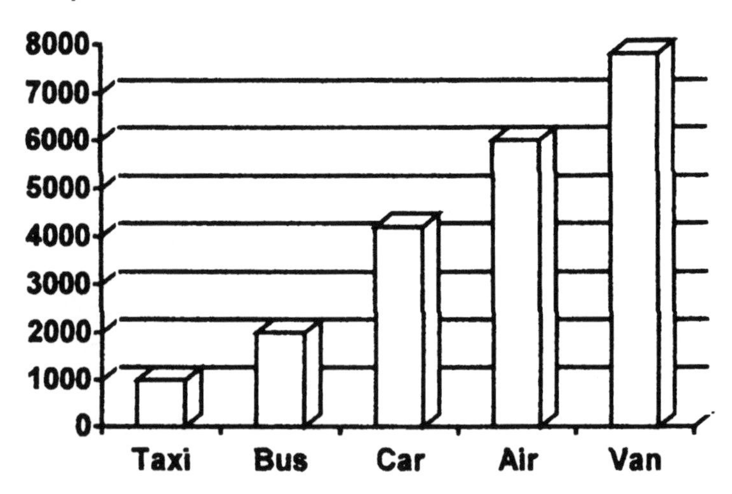

This graph uses bars to show how different quantities compare. The value of bar graphs is that the comparison can be seen at a glance.

Many people traveled to the championship soccer game. The graph shows how many came by taxi, bus, car, airplane, and van. Sample questions:

1. Most people traveled by
   O airplane
   O van
   O taxi
   O car

2. About 4000 people traveled by
   O taxi
   O bus
   O van
   O car

3. More people traveled by bus than by
   O air
   O car
   O taxi
   O van

Line Graph

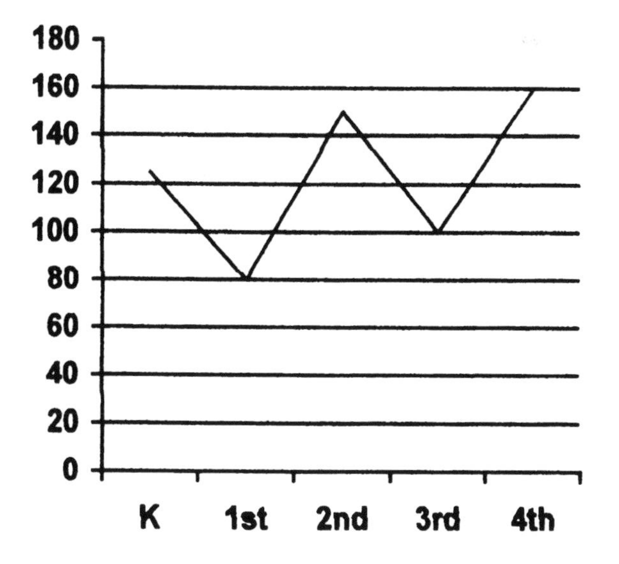

A line graph uses a line to show a pattern of facts. The value of this type of graph is to show upward and downward trends at a glance.

At an elementary school, the number of students at each grade level varies. This type of graph predicts the number of teachers, classrooms, and textbooks needed for the following school year. Sample questions:

1. In what grade level are the most students?
   O 2nd
   O 3rd
   O K
   O 4th

2. How many students began in kindergarten?
   O 175
   O 100
   O 50
   O 125

3. In what grade level are there the fewest students?
   O K
   O 4th
   O 1st
   O 2nd

Pictograph

Rectangle ▭ ▭

Triangle △ △ △

Circle ○ ○ ○ ○

Square □ □ □ □ □

A pictograph uses pictures to show information. Sample questions:

1. Which type of shape was drawn the most?
   O rectangle
   O triangle
   O circle
   O square

2. How many students drew circles?
   O 1
   O 4
   O 2
   O 5

3. Which shape was drawn less often than the triangle?
   O triangle
   O circle
   O rectangle
   O square

Circle (Pie) Graph

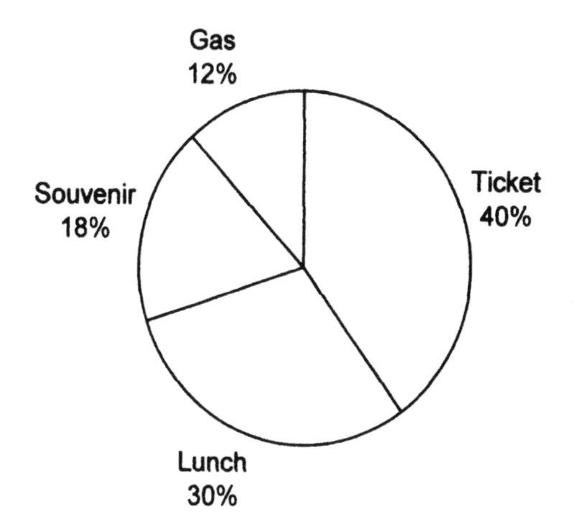

This graph is in the shape of a circle or pie and shows the relationship of the parts to the whole. It is particularly useful when working with budgets. The key indicates what each pattern represents. Each pattern in the graph shows the percent of the total cost for each item.

Each student paid $30.00 to go on the field trip. This graph shows how the expenses were divided. Sample questions:

1. What costs the most?
   O ticket
   O souvenirs
   O lunch
   O gas

2. What item costs less than the souvenirs?
   O lunch
   O gas
   O ticket
   O souvenirs

3. What two items equal over 50 percent of the total cost?
   O lunch and gas
   O gas and souvenir
   O lunch and souvenir
   O ticket and souvenir

Table

Number of Pages Read for Homework

Student	*Reading Pages*	*History Pages*	*Science Pages*	*English Pages*
Ann	10	15	10	4
Bob	5	14	10	4
Cal	25	10	0	4
Donna	12	20	8	2
Ed	15	16	6	2

A table is a chart that contains information about sets of different things. The title of a table shows what the information represents. Sample questions:

1. Which student read the most pages in reading?
   O Ann
   O Bob
   O Ed
   O Cal

2. Who read the least number of pages?
   O Bob
   O Cal
   O Donna
   O Ed

3. How many total pages did Ann and Donna read in history?
   O 25
   O 10
   O 22
   O 35

18

Social Studies, Science, and Reference Skills

Jan gave her dad her latest social studies test on United States history. Dad looked at the D grade and then looked back at his daughter. "Well?" he asked.

"I did all my homework and studied hard," Jan responded defensively. "But when I took the test, my search button didn't work."

Both social studies and science are full subtests in most standardized achievement test batteries. The test-taking strategies for these disciplines are the same as those discussed in chapters 6 to 14 and chapter 16. Even though there are no different test-taking strategies for these subjects, I have included a chapter on them because they are so important to the curriculum and are a part of the total battery score. By combining school textbooks and the strategies in this book, you can effectively teach test-taking strategies for these subjects.

In addition, reference skills are included in many standardized tests, either in the social studies section or in a separate section. The media specialist in your school can help you teach these skills or provide materials for you to use in the classroom. These skills include the use of dictionaries, encyclopedias, atlases, tables of contents and indexes, and card catalogs, as well as other research skills, both in print form and on the Internet.

USING A TABLE OF CONTENTS

Teach this skill when using any textbook in the classroom. Typical questions asked on tests are the following:

1. Which chapter tells about __________?
2. On what page would you begin reading to find out __________?
3. How many pages are in the chapter called __________?
4. To learn _____, on which page will you begin reading?
5. What is the title of the chapter that begins on page __________?
6. Chapter ___ would probably tell about __________.

USING AN INDEX

Use the textbook index often to teach mastery of this skill. Typical questions asked on tests include the following:

1. On what page would you find information about __________?
2. Where will you look to find information about (name of a person)?
3. What pages tell __________?
4. What page gives you the definition of __________?

USING A DICTIONARY

Use a standard dictionary written at the students' level, or use the glossary in the back of the language arts textbook. Ask other teachers if the school has any worn dictionaries they are no longer using, or buy one at the local bookstore. Typical questions asked on standardized tests are as follows:

1. What would describe __________?
2. What is the correct spelling of the word that describes ________?
3. Which of these choices means __________?
4. Which word has __________ syllables?
5. Which word is the opposite of __________?

6. In pronouncing __________, the accent is on the syllable that sounds like __________.
7. Which word is a synonym of __________?
8. Which word is an antonym of __________?

USING AN ENCYCLOPEDIA

Display a set of encyclopedias so that your students can see the volume numbers and the letters of the alphabet. Have students use encyclopedias at the local or school library or one on your computer. Typical questions are as follows:

1. What is the number of the volume you would use to read about __________?
2. Which volume would tell about __________?
3. In which volume might you find information on __________?
4. In which volume would you find a map of __________?
5. Which volume would you use to learn about the culture of __________?

OTHER REFERENCE QUESTIONS

The following are other reference-skill questions that may be found on standardized tests.

1. What is a book of maps called? (atlas)
2. What would you look at to see the shape of the world? (globe)
3. Which book would give the definition of __________? (dictionary)
4. What would best show the route from __________ to __________? (road map)
5. What would you use to learn the history of __________? (encyclopedia)

19

Techniques: The Emotional Factor

I returned to school after the winter holidays with a cast on my left leg because of a broken foot. Patsy, a fifth grader, came into my office to tell me how sorry she was that I was injured. This was a new experience for her, as she had been in my office very often because of bad behavior and work habits. She asked if she could spend the day helping me, running errands and so forth. She stressed that she was good at those things. I thanked her for the offer but told her that she needed to stay in class for the day.

"Why?" she asked. "I wouldn't learn anything anyway." She truly believed this, for that is what her alcoholic father had told her, and her mother never came forth to say otherwise.

At the beginning of this book, I stated the three factors that have a bearing on how successful a student is on a test: 1) knowledge of the material, 2) test anxiety, and 3) test-taking skills (test wiseness) (Divine and Kylen, 1979, vi). Teachers in this nation do a better-than-satisfactory job in teaching basic skills. By also teaching students test-taking strategies, they will help their students become familiar with the test format and thus more comfortable with the testing situation.

However, knowledge of test-taking skills will alleviate only some of the anxiety. The next step is to learn coping skills to deal with the emotions of test taking. Beginning as early as first grade, students need to be taught that tests are just one tool in assessing their achievement or mastery of a subject. Tests are to be respected, not feared.

When I was doing my research for this book, I surveyed the fifth-grade students in my school as to their feelings about tests. I have already shared some of the responses in chapters 10 and 15. Here are some of the other questions and responses:

- ✓ *I would do better on tests if* __________. Most of the answers were related to work and study habits, for example:
  Read the book
  Listen to the teacher
  Study harder
  Do homework
  Do classwork
  Pay attention
- ✓ *I do poorly on tests because I* __________. The responses were overwhelmingly don'ts and were repetitious of the previous answers.
- ✓ *When I take a test, I feel* __________ *because* __________. Most answers as to how the students felt were some sort of anxiety. The "because" answers were in two opposite realms: one from the "A" students who were afraid they would not maintain their A grades, and the other from the poor students who were afraid they would not pass. There were also many students who stated that they were worried that their parents would not love them if they did not do well.

One of the first steps in alleviating anxiety is to discuss with students the reasons tests are given and the many uses for them. At the beginning of the school year, make a chart of these reasons. Examples include the following:

To pass to the next grade
To provide accountability for the teacher, school, and school district
For the teacher to know that the student knows the material
Report card grades
To qualify for special programs (gifted, special education)
To get a driver's license
To get into college and professional schools
To be accepted into the military
To get a professional license
To get a job or a promotion

The rest of this chapter is composed of several activities to help bring students in tune with their feelings about tests and put test taking into a more positive perspective for them.

ACTIVITIES

Activity 1

Give each student a sticky note, and tell them to write one feeling they have had when hearing the word *test*. Each student then says the word and sticks the note on a chart under one of three headings: emotional, physical, or academic. As the students see that their responses mirror their peers' responses, they will feel more free to have a discussion on the subject. There are two rules for this activity: 1) all ideas are worthy, and 2) put-downs are not allowed.

Activity 2

Survey the students with the following questions, adding some of your own. This will also develop into a healthy discussion. Students will be surprised that it is OK to not like tests and it is OK to say so.

1. I would do better on tests if __________.
2. When I take a test, I feel __________ because __________.
3. To get over this feeling, I __________.
4. The worst thing I remember about a test is __________.
5. The best thing I remember about a test is __________.

6. I did by best when __________.
7. I did my poorest when __________.
8. When I take a test, I tell myself __________.

Activity 3
The students will use the survey questions listed in activity 2 to interview three people. One person has to be a parent, one has to be a peer, and the other is the student's choice. I was interviewed several times for this activity. The students will present their responses in an oral class activity. The object is to bring to the students' attention the fact that many others have the same feelings about taking tests.

Activity 4
Have students write a letter to the school principal, their state or federal representatives (they are making many of the laws requiring testing), or the school superintendent stating their opinion about tests and why or why not to eliminate or curtail them from the school district's curriculum.

Activity 5
Make a chart using the words from all the surveys in activity 2 concerning the feelings about tests. Discuss why people might have those feelings, and then list ways to alleviate them.

Activity 6
Have students write a poem about tests.

Activity 7
Have students write a letter to the editor of the local newspaper expressing their opinions about tests and relating how elementary school students feel about them.

Activity 8
Have students write a story: "How I Sent My Test-Taking Worries into Space!"

Activity 9

Have the class work together to compose a letter to the publisher of the school's standardized test. Have students tell the good things about their test as well as the bad things, and have them tell how the publisher can make the test better for the students. Also have students ask the publisher how tests are made. A representative of the publisher may even visit the class.

20

Writing

When my son was in fourth grade, he came home from school one Friday clutching his writing folder. He had a great big smile on his face. I immediately became suspicious, for he did not like school. "Did you know there is a different system for grading stories?" he asked. "Oh?" I replied with a great deal of skepticism. "Yes!" he said excitedly. "A means awful, B means bad, C means careful, D means dandy, and F means fantastic." I gave him credit for being creative, and his work was much better than I had expected.

Since that time, writing has taken on a whole new role in the elementary curriculum. Teachers are now taught in depth to teach writing skills to elementary school students, beginning as early as kindergarten. This change was needed after a period inundated with workbooks, dittos, and black-line masters in which the student simply filled in the blanks. Students were not required to write complete sentences or paragraphs. The pendulum has swung back, as it periodically does in the field of education. Computers do not have blanks to be filled in: users are required to create and compose their thoughts when using the keyboard. Writing has become a priority and a necessity. Students must not only do well throughout the school year, they must also demonstrate their mastery of writing skills, which are generally tested in the fourth grade in the elementary sequence.

The scores on these tests are used to rate teachers, schools, and school systems. But the positive side is that teachers are being trained to teach writing skills, and as a result, students are becoming proficient writers.

States have put together task teams to write the criteria and prompts for the tests. Teachers and other educators have been selected and put through a training regimen to score writing tests according to a specific set of guidelines.

Most states require writing tests of fourth graders. However, the teaching of writing skills needs to be introduced in the beginning years of the elementary curriculum. There are four factors to be considered when teaching writing:

1. The genre of the written work
2. The elements of the work
3. The rubric (scoring) of the work
4. Activities for students in preparing for the tests

Each state has its own specific guidelines. A copy of these guidelines should be made available to every teacher. Some score on a scale of 1 to 6, and others grade on a scale of 1 to 4. The rubrics are the same; the difference is the gradation of the skills for each score. The information in this chapter applies to all writing tests.

THE GENRE OF THE WRITTEN WORK

Children write for a variety of reasons. The genres for writing tests seem to fall into three categories. Some states ask students to write on two different genres. In some cases, the students in a classroom are not all given the same writing assignment.

1. Informative, expository, open-ended, or open response: The student is expected to write to inform, clarify, define, explain, instruct, or report. A specific prompt is given to the students asking

them to write in a variety of formats. The writing may be composed in the form of a report, a letter, a review, or an essay.
2. Narrative, on-demand writing: This genre is either factual or fictional and takes the form of a story. The student is asked to write about an experience or event.
3. Persuasive writing: The student in this case endeavors to influence the reader to take some sort of action. This action may be change, improvements, permissions granted, or support for activities. Since the writer is persuading, the composition may contain reasons, documentation, examples, and comparisons.

THE ELEMENTS OF THE WORK

Holistic scoring is the process by which writing compositions are graded. This means that no one element has a greater weight than another element. The scorer looks at the work as a whole, not in separate parts. The thoroughness with which four elements are incorporated into the work is the criteria on which the rubric score is based.

1. Focus: Focus refers to how well the writer stays on topic without digressing. The subject has to be consistently and clearly maintained.
2. Organization: The organization is the plan of development, including a logical sequence of events. There has to be a very clear beginning, middle, and conclusion. Organization is evidenced by transitions from one thought to the next and the inclusion of supporting ideas.
3. Support: Support refers to all the details that enhance the topic. There are words that define, clarify, and explain. There is strong evidence of a varied vocabulary and mature word choice.
4. Conventions: Conventions are the English skills:
    - ✓ Spelling
    - ✓ Punctuation
    - ✓ Capitalization

- ✓ Legible handwriting
- ✓ Complete sentence structure, including simple, compound, and complex sentences
- ✓ Noun and verb agreement

THE RUBRIC OF THE WORK

A rubric is a set of scoring criteria at each point on a scale, just as grades (A, B, C) or percentages (80%, 85%, 90%) are used in the classroom. The following is a guide to a four-point-scale rubric. A six-point-scale rubric evaluates the same skills but applies a finer division in the application of the elements.

Rubric 4

- ✓ Focus on the topic is complete and clear.
- ✓ Sequence flows logically from beginning to end.
- ✓ There is a sense of completeness.
- ✓ Vocabulary and sentence structure are effective and varied.
- ✓ The work shows an awareness of correct parts of speech and spelling.
- ✓ Correct punctuation and capitalization are used.

Rubric 3

All of the above skills are displayed adequately with minor errors.

Rubric 2

- ✓ The writer adequately focuses on the prompt.
- ✓ There is evidence of digressing and extraneous material.
- ✓ There are some supporting details, but support is not complete.
- ✓ There is a loose attempt at sequence.
- ✓ Vocabulary and sentence structure are limited.
- ✓ Errors are evident in spelling, capitalization, and punctuation.

Rubric 1

The paper is poorly written with frequent and glaring errors in all areas. Focus on the topic is lacking.

ACTIVITIES

1. In class, assign a prompt and allow the same amount of time that will be allowed for the test.
2. Grade students' writing in the rubric format. Explain this system to students. The school system's writing coordinator can provide guidelines for teachers as to how to score writing using this system.
3. Allow students to suggest prompts.
4. Make charts of descriptive words (adverbs and adjectives).
5. Have students practice varying the vocabulary used in their writing.
6. Provide models of all levels of writing. The school's or school system's writing coordinator should be able to provide samples.
7. Have students practice writing. Use the following sample ideas:
   - ✓ Show the students a picture from the local newspaper. Ask them to write a story to accompany the picture.
   - ✓ Have students write a review of a school assembly, play, or concert.
   - ✓ Take a picture of a school activity and ask students to write a story about it.
   - ✓ Have students write a story about why homework is necessary.
   - ✓ Have students write a letter to the principal requesting changes in a policy or procedure.
   - ✓ Have students write a letter to the testing company stating their opinions about tests.
   - ✓ Have students write about a favorite day or event.
   - ✓ Have students write a letter to their parent or guardian asking for permission to do something.

✓ Have students write about their favorite time of year.
✓ Have students describe their favorite room in the house through the five senses.
✓ Require students to keep a daily journal.

DEFINITIONS RELATED TO WRITING TESTS

Conventions: The commonly accepted and appropriate rules of English spelling, capitalization, and punctuation.
Draft: The first version of a writing piece before revisions.
Expository/open-ended/informative writing: Writing that explains, clarifies, defines, teaches, and generally gives information.
Focus: The point of concentration on the topic.
Holistic scoring: A method of evaluating a composition as to its overall quality.
Narrative/on-demand writing: Factual or fictional writing that tells a story sequentially.
Organization: Development of beginning/middle/end and the process used to progress from one thought to the next.
Persuasive writing: Writing that attempts to motivate a reader to a specific action or viewpoint.
Prompt: A writing assignment that directs the writer to a specific topic.
Rubric: A set of criteria for each score point of a scale.
Support: Evidence and facts pointing to the central topic of a piece of writing.

IV

STOP

21

Everyone's Role: Teacher, Parent, Student

FOR THE TEACHER

1. Read and reread the test manual.
2. Use practice worksheets in daily classwork that are written in testing format.
3. Give students a stretch break or rest between parts of the test.
4. Put a "Testing—Do Not Disturb" sign on the door so that there will be no interruptions.
5. Notify the office of the times there are to be no interruptions: no intercom, no parents, no late students. Tell students prior to the test that no one will be admitted to the classroom once the test has begun.
6. Make no changes in the classroom the week before the test to eliminate new distractions: do not rearrange furniture, do not change bulletin boards, and even do not wear a new outfit or hairdo.
7. Give practice tests throughout the school year.
8. Take notes the day of the test. Was the student ill, did the student's dog die, or was there an upsetting family incident that morning?
9. Explain to students why they are taking this particular test.

10. Tell students when the results will be available and who will get them.
11. Explain to students whether the test is written in such a way that some of the material might be too difficult for them.
12. Explain how the results will be used.
13. Explain how makeups will be handled.
14. State whether or not the test is timed, and for how long.
15. State whether or not the teacher can answer questions once the test has begun.
16. Explain any specific procedures in the manual, for example, the directions must be read exactly as stated, both in the wording and how many times the teacher is allowed to read the directions; times will be strictly adhered to; and students may not go back to a previous section or look ahead to the next section.
17. Tell students what to do if
    - their pencil breaks.
    - they have physical problems, such as a cough, a headache, or any other illness.
    - they have made a mistake and want to change an answer.
    - they finish before time is up.
18. Take care of bathroom needs before the test begins, and announce that no one is allowed to leave the room once the test has started.

FOR THE PARENT

Ask the teacher to explain the following:

✓ What tests are given
✓ When the tests are given
✓ Why the tests are given
✓ When they can expect their child's results
✓ Definitions of terms they need to know in order to understand the results

To help parents support their student, teachers should provide parents with guidelines on the basics:

- ✓ Sleep: See that the child goes to bed at his or her regular time. Too much sleep is just as detrimental as too little sleep.
- ✓ Breakfast: See that the child eats his or her regular breakfast. However, children who do not usually eat breakfast should eat something on the day of the test.
- ✓ Clothing: See that the child wears comfortable clothing and also the clothing that is his or her favorite. Check the weather for the day.
- ✓ Materials: Provide the child with two number-two pencils and an eraser.
- ✓ Be on the child's side: Send the child to school knowing that you want the child to do his or her best and that you will support the results.

FOR THE STUDENT

1. Come to the test prepared:
    - Bring two number-two pencils and an eraser.
    - Take care of bathroom needs before the test.
    - Have tissues handy.
    - Wear comfortable clothing (check the weather).
    - Get enough rest for you to be able to do your best work.
    - Eat breakfast to meet your needs.
2. Are you a tortoise or a hare? (To the teacher: Read the story to the class and discuss the traits of each and the advantages and disadvantages of working too slowly or too fast.)
3. Use your guessing skills.
4. Read everything carefully.
5. Read questions twice.
6. Follow the directions exactly.
7. Use your time wisely.
8. Remember WATCH. (See chapter 1.)
9. Do the best you can do!

22

Wind Down and Wrap Up

I'm a list maker and list user. It's the easiest way for me to ensure that I have covered all the necessary information. I have made two checklists for this purpose: one for the test giver and the other for students. The items on these lists help set the tone for a positive and productive testing situation.

FOR THE TEST GIVER

1. Read the manual prior to the testing situation, at least twice, so that you know exactly what to say, how many times to say it, and what is timed. (See the explanations of test directions in appendix G.)
2. Set the school telephone and all cell phones to "off."
3. Put a sign on the classroom door: "Testing—Do Not Disturb."
4. Make sure students understand the directions and what help can and cannot be given.
5. Check the answer sheet of each student who has finished and point to the number of any unanswered questions. Usually this is all the help you are allowed to give.
6. Remind students that they may not know all the answers, especially on national achievement tests.

7. Post a chart in the classroom of the testing rules (appendix D), and review the rules before every test.
8. Remind students to read the entire question and all answer choices before selecting their answer.
9. Have extra number-two pencils and erasers handy. I cannot stress this enough.
10. Remind students that if they change their answer, they must erase the first choice completely.
11. If a change in room arrangement is needed, do it at least a week prior to the testing day.
12. Give stretch breaks and bathroom breaks between sections, if needed.
13. Assure students that they are expected to do their best; alleviate as much pressure as possible.

FOR THE STUDENT

1. Read the question and all answer choices before marking the selection.
2. Look for the math sign before completing the problem.
3. Look for key words in the questions that give clues to the answer.
4. Check to make sure all questions are answered.
5. Guess the answers to questions you do not know, using your guessing skills.
6. Watch the time: don't be a tortoise or a hare.
7. Don't spend a lot of time on one question; skip it and come back to it if time allows. Remember to skip the line on the answer sheet also.
8. For fill-in-the-blank questions, try each answer choice to see which makes the most sense.
9. Expect only one correct answer.
10. Expect no pattern to the answers, such as A B C A B C.

11. Don't worry about the other students.
12. Come prepared with two number-two pencils and an eraser. Again, this is very important.
13. Dress comfortably and for the weather.
14. Read the directions twice.
15. Even if you are sure of the answer on a reading comprehension test, go back and find it in the passage.
16. Do the best you can!

Appendix A: Definitions of Testing Terms

Achievement test: A test that measures the extent to which a student has attained specific information or mastered specific skills
Battery: A group of several tests (encompassing the grade-level curriculum) that have been standardized on the same population so that results of the tests are comparable. The most common test batteries are those of achievement tests, which include subtests in all areas of the curriculum.
Composite score: A score that combines several scores
Correlation: The relationship between two sets of scores or measures
Criterion-referenced test: A test that measures specific knowledge or skills of the student. A criterion-referenced test does not rank students against each other or tell if the student is on grade level; it simply tests whether the child has mastered specific skills.
Diagnostic test: A test used to diagnose or analyze a student's specific areas of strength or weakness
Distracter: Any incorrect answer choice in a test
Grade equivalent: The grade level for which a given score is the real or estimated average
Item analysis: The process of evaluating individual test items with respect to certain characteristics
Mean: The mean of a set of scores is the average of the scores.

Median: When scores are ranked from high to low, the median is the middle score.

Norm-referenced test: This type of test measures what the student knows, compares the student to students of the same age or grade level around the country, and ranks the student against peers.

Norms: Norms are results based on the actual performance of pupils of various grades or ages in the standardized group for the test.

Objective test: A test scored with a key and consisting of items for which correct responses are determined in advance

Percentile: A ranking in a distribution of scores. For example, a percentile of 85 means that 85 percent of the students who took the test in question scored lower than the student in question. Of every hundred students who took the test in the United States, eighty-four scored lower than the test taker.

Profile: A graphic representation of a student's results on a test. A quick look at a profile will show strengths and weaknesses.

Quartile: When a set of test scores is divided equally into four groups, each group is a quartile, with the top quartile (75th percentile to 100th percentile) being the best and the bottom (1st percentile to 25th percentile) being the students who need help.

Random sample: A sample of members of a total population chosen in such a way that every member of the population has an equal chance of being included

Raw score: The number of correct answers, or, in the case of some tests, the number of correct answers minus the number of wrong answers

Reliability: The extent to which a test measures what it says it is going to measure and is consistent with this measure

Standard score: The difference between the raw score and the mean, divided by the standard deviation. An example of the classification of standard scores is as follows: Very superior: 130 and up; Superior: 120–129; High average: 110–119; Average: 90–109; Low average: 80–89; Borderline: 70–79; Deficient: 69 and below.

Standardized tests: Tests that have the same questions and the same directions for administration, are given in the same setting, and are scored in conformance with definite rules

Stanine: One of the steps in a nine-point scale of standard scores, for example, Low: 1, 2, 3; Average: 4, 5, 6; High: 7, 8, 9

Validity: The extent to which a test measures what the teacher taught

Appendix B: Sample Test Answer Sheet

1. A B C D E
2. A B C D E
3. A B C D E
4. A B C D E
5. A B C D E
6. A B C D E
7. A B C D E
8. A B C D E
9. A B C D E
10. A B C D E
11. A B C D E
12. A B C D E
13. A B C D E
14. A B C D E
15. A B C D E
16. A B C D E
17. A B C D E
18. A B C D E
19. A B C D E
20. A B C D E
21. A B C D
22. A B C D
23. A B C D
24. A B C D
25. A B C D

1. A B C D E
2. A B C D E
3. A B C D E
4. A B C D E
5. A B C D E
6. A B C D E
7. A B C D E
8. A B C D E
9. A B C D E
10. A B C D E
11. A B C D E
12. A B C D E
13. A B C D E
14. A B C D E
15. A B C D E
16. A B C D E
17. A B C D E
18. A B C D E
19. A B C D E
20. A B C D E
21. A B C D E
22. A B C D E
23. A B C D E
24. A B C D E
25. A B C D E

1. A B C D E
2. A B C D E
3. A B C D E
4. A B C D E
5. A B C D E
6. A B C D E
7. A B C D E
8. A B C D E
9. A B C D E
10. A B C D E
11. A B C D E
12. A B C D E
13. A B C D E
14. A B C D E
15. A B C D E
16. A B C D E
17. A B C D E
18. A B C D E
19. A B C D E
20. A B C D E
21. A B C D E
22. A B C D E
23. A B C D E
24. A B C D E
25. A B C D E
26. A B C D E
27. A B C D E
28. A B C D E
29. A B C D E
30. A B C D E
31. A B C D E
32. A B C D E
33. A B C D E
34. A B C D E
35. A B C D E
36. A B C D E
37. A B C D E
38. A B C D E
39. A B C D E
40. A B C D E
41. A B C D E
42. A B C D E
43. A B C D E
44. A B C D E
45. A B C D E
46. A B C D E
47. A B C D E
48. A B C D E
49. A B C D E
50. A B C D E

Appendix C: Game Chart

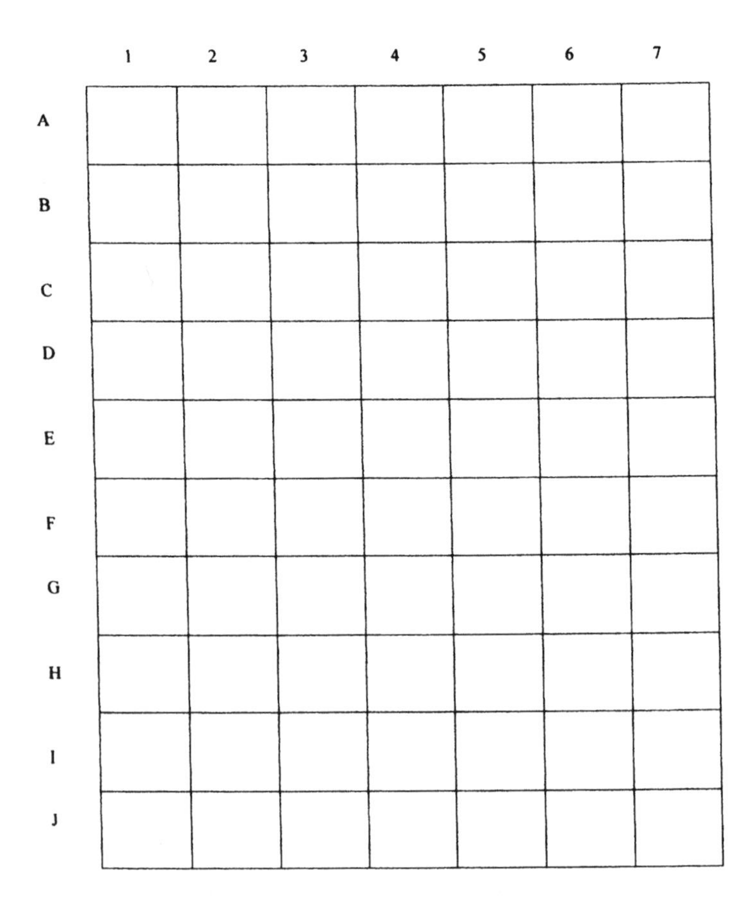

Appendix D: Rules for Taking Tests

At the beginning of the school year, first discuss the types of tests required throughout the year. Then, as each testing date approaches, discuss with students the test to be given. Before each test, discuss the following rules and explain how each will help the student to meet with success.

1. I will read the directions carefully.
2. I will read the test questions carefully.
3. I will follow directions exactly.
4. I will mark each answer fully and match the item number to the answer number.
5. I will erase completely if I change an answer.
6. I will begin when I am told to do so.
7. I will stop when I am told to do so.
8. If I am having problems, I will quietly raise my hand and wait for help.
9. I will dress comfortably and appropriately for the weather.
10. I will bring the materials I need: two number-two pencils and an eraser.
11. I will not pay attention to others while I am taking the test.
12. I will not read out loud.
13. When I finish, I will be very quiet until everyone else finishes.
14. I will do the best I can!

Appendix E: Suggested Weekly Lesson Plan

MONDAY

Select your skill of the week, and, using the students' materials, write out two sample test questions. Work on these two sample questions step-by-step with the students.

For example, tell students to read the test questions, and then tell them to read the corresponding passage in their book (reading textbook, library book, social studies book). Read the passage to students, alternate reading the passage with students, or have students read it aloud to you. Ask the following question: What is the main idea of the passage?

Discuss each of the four answer choices. Together discuss why each is a good choice or why it does not answer the question. Repeat this activity with a different passage and a different set of answer choices.

TUESDAY

Follow the same format as Monday using a different source. If the reading text was used Monday, select passages from the social studies or science text on Tuesday.

WEDNESDAY

Follow the same format as Monday and Tuesday, using different material. This time, let students tell you why each answer choice is right or inappropriate.

THURSDAY

Repeat Wednesday's format.

FRIDAY

Repeat the format from Monday, but have students do the work independently. Check students' work for mastery of the skill. Discuss the results with students.

Appendix F: Daily Lesson Plan

Day: ___________ Date: _______ Subject Area: _______________

Skill: ____

Textbook: __________________________ Pages: ______________

Sample test items

Question: ____

____

A. ____
B. ____
C. ____
D. ____

Question:____

____

A. ____
B. ____
C. ____
D. ____

Appendix G: Definitions of Test Directions

Bubble in, fill in, darken, mark: All four terms mean the same thing, that is, to indicate with a pencil on a machine-readable form which answer the tester has chosen.
Compare: Point out the likenesses of the items in question.
Contrast: Point out the differences between the items in question.
Define: Give the meaning or synonym of a term.
Describe: Tell the physical characteristics of the item in question.
Estimate: Give an approximate value, generally in math.
Explain: Give reasons, particularly regarding causes, motivation, and so forth.
Illustrate: Give specific examples, or draw a diagram or picture.
List: Make a list.
Prove: Show that something is true by giving specific examples.
Read the article/passage/selection/story: Read all the words on the page between the directions and the question. All four words mean the same thing in this context.
State: This direction may also be written as "state the reasons for" or "give the reasons for" and it requires a written response. This direction is not used in tests that are completely scored by a scanner.
Summarize: Briefly state the main points; do not give many details.
Tell about: Write a narrative story about the specified subject.

References

Alford, Robert L. 1979. *Tips on Testing: Strategies for Test Taking.* Washington, DC: University Press of America.

Burrill, Lois E. 1981. "How a Standardized Achievement Test Is Built." *Test Service Notebook 125.* New York: Psychological Corporation.

Divine, James H., and David W. Kylen. 1979. *How to Beat Test Anxiety.* New York: Barron's Educational Series.

Durham, Guinevere. 2003. *Surviving Today's Schools: The Inside Story.* Baltimore: Publish America.

Feder, Bernard. 1979. *The Complete Guide to Taking Tests.* Englewood Cliffs, NJ: Prentice-Hall.

Florida Department of Education. 1981. *Item Development Workshop.* Tallahassee: State of Florida, Department of State.

Lang, Bob. 1981. "Promoting Test-Wiseness." *Journal of Reading 24* (8): 740–42.

Scruggs, Thomas E., and Margo A. Mastropieri. 1992. *Teaching Test-Taking Skills.* Cambridge, MA: Brookline Books.

About the Author

Guinevere Durham has been described by one of her teachers as an "advocate of children." She has spent thirty years in every aspect of elementary and early childhood education, confronting challenges and reaping blessings. She also was a willing participant in the educational and social activities of her six children. Her education and experiences instilled in her the need to help both teachers and children, thus, the purpose for *Teaching Test-Taking Skills.*

Durham has won national awards as a teacher of the year and educator of the year. In addition, she was recognized for her teacher workshops and conference presentations in the fields of parenting, school improvement, and test-taking strategies. Her contributions to publishers of reading textbooks and Sunday school curricula benefited teachers in their efforts to help students. As a retired elementary principal with bachelor's and master's degrees in elementary education and a doctorate in early childhood education, she has qualified for listings in three different *Who's Whos* in education during her career.

Made in the USA
San Bernardino, CA
04 January 2019